Teach Yourself
VISUALLY™
Windows® *Me*
Millennium Edition

Visual™

From
maranGraphics™

&

IDG BOOKS

IDG Books Worldwide, Inc.
An International Data Group Company
Foster City, CA • Indianapolis • Chicago • New York

Teach Yourself VISUALLY™ Windows® Me Millennium Edition

Published by
IDG Books Worldwide, Inc.
An International Data Group Company
919 E. Hillsdale Blvd., Suite 400
Foster City, CA 94404

Library of Congress Catalog Card No.: 00-103129

ISBN: 0-7645-3495-5

Printed in the United States of America

10 9 8 7 6 5 4 3 2 1

1K/SZ/QX/QQ/MG

Distributed in the United States by IDG Books Worldwide, Inc.

Distributed by CDG Books Canada Inc. for Canada; by Transworld Publishers Limited in the United Kingdom; by IDG Norge Books for Norway; by IDG Sweden Books for Sweden; by IDG Books Australia Publishing Corporation Pty. Ltd. for Australia and New Zealand; by TransQuest Publishers Pte Ltd. for Singapore, Malaysia, Thailand, Indonesia, and Hong Kong; by Gotop Information Inc. for Taiwan; by ICG Muse, Inc. for Japan; by Intersoft for South Africa; by Eyrolles for France; by International Thomson Publishing for Germany, Austria and Switzerland; by Distribuidora Cuspide for Argentina; by LR International for Brazil; by Galileo Libros for Chile; by Ediciones ZETA S.C.R. Ltda. for Peru; by WS Computer Publishing Corporation, Inc. for the Philippines; by Contemporanea de Ediciones for Venezuela; by Express Computer Distributors for the Caribbean and West Indies; by Micronesia Media Distributor, Inc. for Micronesia; by Chips Computadoras S.A. de C.V. for Mexico; by Editorial Norma de Panama S.A. for Panama; by American Bookshops for Finland.

For corporate orders, please call maranGraphics at 800-469-6616.
For general information on IDG Books Worldwide's books in the U.S., please call our Consumer Customer Service department at 800-762-2974.
For reseller information, including discounts and premium sales, please call our Reseller Customer Service department at 800-434-3422.
For information on where to purchase IDG Books Worldwide's books outside the U.S., please contact our International Sales department at 317-572-3993 or fax 317-572-4002.
For consumer information on foreign language translations, please contact our Customer Service department at 800-434-3422, fax 800-550-2747, or e-mail rights@idgbooks.com.
For information on licensing foreign or domestic rights, please phone 650-653-7000 or fax 650-653-7500.
For sales inquiries and special prices for bulk quantities, please contact our Sales department at 650-655-3200.
For information on using IDG Books Worldwide's books in the classroom or for ordering examination copies, please contact our Educational Sales department at 800-434-2086 or fax 317-572-4005.
For press review copies, author interviews, or other publicity information, please contact our Public Relations department at 650-653-7000 or fax 650-653-7500.
For authorization to photocopy items for corporate, personal, or educational use, please contact maranGraphics at 800-469-6616.

Trademark Acknowledgments

Permissions

© 2000 maranGraphics, Inc.

The 3-D illustrations are the copyright of maranGraphics, Inc.

U.S. Corporate Sales	U.S. Trade Sales
Contact maranGraphics at (800) 469-6616 or Fax (905) 890-9434.	Contact IDG Books at (800) 434-3422 or (650) 653-7000.

ABOUT IDG BOOKS WORLDWIDE

Welcome to the world of IDG Books Worldwide.

IDG Books Worldwide, Inc., is a subsidiary of International Data Group, the world's largest publisher of computer-related information and the leading global provider of information services on information technology. IDG was founded more than 30 years ago by Patrick J. McGovern and now employs more than 9,000 people worldwide. IDG publishes more than 290 computer publications in over 75 countries. More than 90 million people read one or more IDG publications each month.

Launched in 1990, IDG Books Worldwide is today the #1 publisher of best-selling computer books in the United States. We are proud to have received eight awards from the Computer Press Association in recognition of editorial excellence and three from Computer Currents' First Annual Readers' Choice Awards. Our best-selling ...*For Dummies*® series has more than 50 million copies in print with translations in 31 languages. IDG Books Worldwide, through a joint venture with IDG's Hi-Tech Beijing, became the first U.S. publisher to publish a computer book in the People's Republic of China. In record time, IDG Books Worldwide has become the first choice for millions of readers around the world who want to learn how to better manage their businesses.

Our mission is simple: Every one of our books is designed to bring extra value and skill-building instructions to the reader. Our books are written by experts who understand and care about our readers. The knowledge base of our editorial staff comes from years of experience in publishing, education, and journalism — experience we use to produce books to carry us into the new millennium. In short, we care about books, so we attract the best people. We devote special attention to details such as audience, interior design, use of icons, and illustrations. And because we use an efficient process of authoring, editing, and desktop publishing our books electronically, we can spend more time ensuring superior content and less time on the technicalities of making books.

You can count on our commitment to deliver high-quality books at competitive prices on topics you want to read about. At IDG Books Worldwide, we continue in the IDG tradition of delivering quality for more than 30 years. You'll find no better book on a subject than one from IDG Books Worldwide.

John Kilcullen
Chairman and CEO
IDG Books Worldwide, Inc.

Eighth Annual Computer Press Awards ≥ 1992

Ninth Annual Computer Press Awards ≥ 1993

Tenth Annual Computer Press Awards ≥ 1994

Eleventh Annual Computer Press Awards ≥ 1995

IDG is the world's leading IT media, research and exposition company. Founded in 1964, IDG had 1997 revenues of $2.05 billion and has more than 9,000 employees worldwide. IDG offers the widest range of media options that reach IT buyers in 75 countries representing 95% of worldwide IT spending. IDG's diverse product and services portfolio spans six key areas including print publishing, online publishing, expositions and conferences, market research, education and training, and global marketing services. More than 90 million people read one or more of IDG's 290 magazines and newspapers, including IDG's leading global brands — Computerworld, PC World, Network World, Macworld and the Channel World family of publications. IDG Books Worldwide is one of the fastest-growing computer book publishers in the world, with more than 700 titles in 36 languages. The "...For Dummies®" series alone has more than 50 million copies in print. IDG offers online users the largest network of technology-specific Web sites around the world through IDG.net (http://www.idg.net), which comprises more than 225 targeted Web sites in 55 countries worldwide. International Data Corporation (IDC) is the world's largest provider of information technology data, analysis and consulting, with research centers in over 41 countries and more than 400 research analysts worldwide. IDG World Expo is a leading producer of more than 168 globally branded conferences and expositions in 35 countries including E3 (Electronic Entertainment Expo), Macworld Expo, ComNet, Windows World Expo, ICE (Internet Commerce Expo), Agenda, DEMO, and Spotlight. IDG's training subsidiary, ExecuTrain, is the world's largest computer training company, with more than 230 locations worldwide and 785 training courses. IDG Marketing Services helps industry-leading IT companies build international brand recognition by developing global integrated marketing programs via IDG's print, online and exposition products worldwide. Further information about the company can be found at www.idg.com. 1/26/00

maranGraphics is a family-run business
located near Toronto, Canada.

At **maranGraphics**, we believe in producing great computer books–one book at a time.

Each maranGraphics book uses the award-winning communication process that we have been developing over the last 25 years. Using this process, we organize screen shots, text and illustrations in a way that makes it easy for you to learn new concepts and tasks.

We spend hours deciding the best way to perform each task, so you don't have to! Our clear, easy-to-follow screen shots and instructions walk you through each task from beginning to end.

Our detailed illustrations go hand-in-hand with the text to help reinforce the information. Each illustration is a labor of love–some take up to a week to draw!

We want to thank you for purchasing what we feel are the best computer books money can buy. We hope you enjoy using this book as much as we enjoyed creating it!

Sincerely,

The Maran Family

Please visit us on the Web at:
www.maran.com

CREDITS

Author:
Ruth Maran

Copy Editors:
Raquel Scott
Jill Maran

Technical Consultant:
Paul Whitehead

Project Manager:
Judy Maran

Editors:
Teri Lynn Pinsent
Luis Lee
Janice Boyer

Screen Captures & Editing:
James Menzies

Layout Designer:
Treena Lees

Illustrators:
Russ Marini
Sean Johannesen
Steven Schaerer
Ted Sheppard

Screen Artist & Illustrator:
Jimmy Tam

Indexer:
Raquel Scott

Permissions Coordinator:
Jennifer Amaral

Post Production:
Robert Maran

**Senior Vice President,
Technology Publishing
IDG Books Worldwide:**
Richard Swadley

**Editorial Support
IDG Books Worldwide:**
Barry Pruett
Martine Edwards

ACKNOWLEDGMENTS

Thanks to the dedicated staff of maranGraphics, including
Jennifer Amaral, Roderick Anatalio, Cathy Benn,
Sean Johannesen, Kelleigh Johnson, Eric Kramer, Wanda Lawrie,
Luis Lee, Treena Lees, Jill Maran, Judy Maran, Robert Maran,
Russ Marini, James Menzies, Suzana Miokovic, Stacey Morrison,
Teri Lynn Pinsent, Steven Schaerer, Raquel Scott, Ted Sheppard,
Jimmy Tam, Roxanne Van Damme and Paul Whitehead.

Finally, to Richard Maran who originated the easy-to-use
graphic format of this guide. Thank you for your
inspiration and guidance.

TABLE OF CONTENTS

Chapter 1

WINDOWS BASICS

Chapter 2

CREATE DOCUMENTS

Chapter 3

CREATE PICTURES

Chapter 4

VIEW FILES

Chapter 5

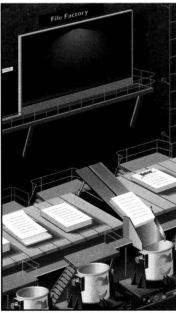

WORK WITH FILES

TABLE OF CONTENTS

Chapter 6

CUSTOMIZE WINDOWS

Chapter 7

HAVE FUN WITH WINDOWS

Chapter 8

CREATE MOVIES

Chapter 9

OPTIMIZE YOUR COMPUTER

TABLE OF CONTENTS

Chapter 12

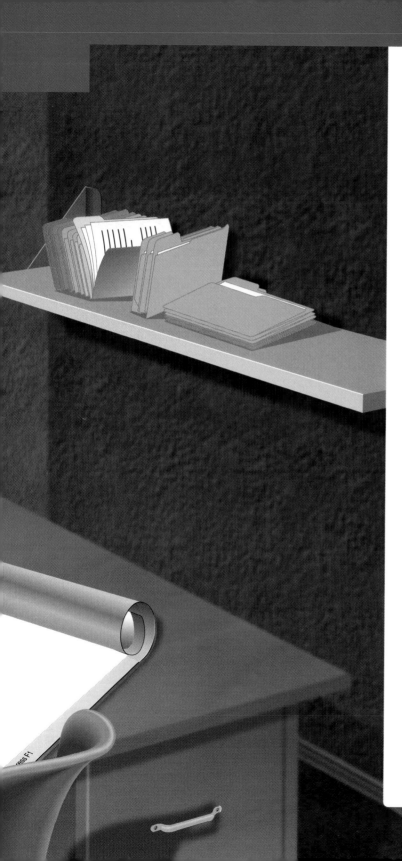

CHAPTER 1

Windows Basics

Welcome to Windows Me! In this chapter you will learn all the basic skills that you will need to operate Windows Me.

INTRODUCTION TO WINDOWS

Microsoft®
Windows® Me
is a program
that controls the
overall activity
of your computer.

Microsoft
Windows Me
ensures that all
parts of your
computer work
together smoothly
and efficiently.

WORK WITH FILES

Windows provides ways to organize and manage the files stored on your computer. You can open, sort, rename, move, print, search for and delete files.

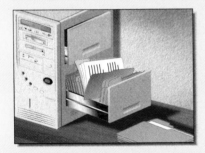

Windows includes the WordPad and Paint programs to help you quickly start creating files. WordPad is a simple word processing program and Paint is a simple drawing program.

CUSTOMIZE WINDOWS

You can customize Windows to suit your preferences. You can add a colorful design to your screen, change the amount of information that fits on your screen and change the way your mouse works.

HAVE FUN WITH WINDOWS

You can play games, listen to music CDs, play sound effects when you perform certain tasks and listen to radio station broadcasts on the Internet. You can also transfer your home movies to your computer and then organize and edit the movies before sharing them with friends and family.

OPTIMIZE YOUR COMPUTER

Windows provides tools to help you optimize your computer. You can check your hard disk for errors, install new programs, remove unnecessary files to free up disk space and restore your computer if you experience problems.

WORK ON A NETWORK

Windows allows you to share information and equipment with other people on a network. You can share folders stored on your computer as well as a printer that is directly connected to your computer. Windows provides a wizard to help you set up a network at home.

BROWSE THE WEB

Windows allows you to browse through the vast amount of information available on the World Wide Web. You can move between Web pages you have viewed, search for Web pages of interest and create a list of your favorite Web pages so you can quickly return to the pages.

EXCHANGE ELECTRONIC MAIL

Windows allows you to exchange electronic mail with people around the world. You can read, send, reply to, forward, print and delete e-mail messages. You can also use the address book to store the e-mail addresses of people you frequently send messages to.

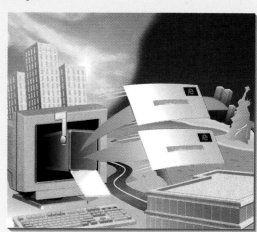

PARTS OF THE WINDOWS SCREEN

DESKTOP

The background area of your screen.

TITLE BAR

Displays the name of an open window.

WINDOW

A rectangle on your screen that displays information.

MY DOCUMENTS

Provides a convenient place to store your documents.

MY COMPUTER

Allows you to view all the folders and files stored on your computer.

MY NETWORK PLACES

Allows you to view the folders and files available on your network.

RECYCLE BIN

Stores deleted files and allows you to recover them later.

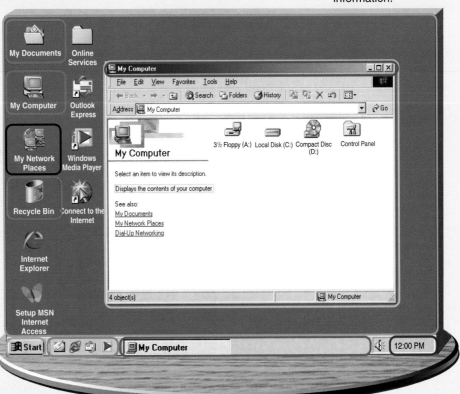

START BUTTON

Provides quick access to programs, files and help with Windows.

QUICK LAUNCH TOOLBAR

Provides quick access to commonly used features.

🔲 Allows you to temporarily remove all open windows so you can clearly view the desktop.

🔳 Allows you to access information on the Web.

🔳 Allows you to exchange electronic mail.

▶ Allows you to play sounds and videos.

TASKBAR

Displays a button for each open window on your screen. You can use these buttons to switch between open windows.

CLOCK

Displays the current time.

USING THE MOUSE

A mouse is a handheld device that allows you to select and move items on your screen.

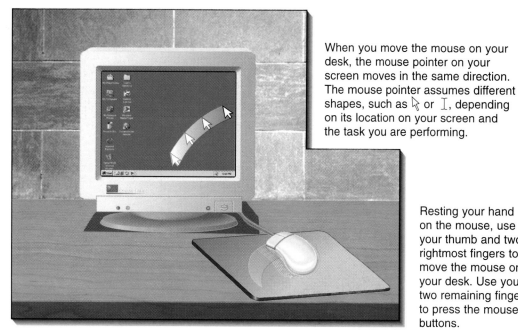

When you move the mouse on your desk, the mouse pointer on your screen moves in the same direction. The mouse pointer assumes different shapes, such as ⍨ or I, depending on its location on your screen and the task you are performing.

Resting your hand on the mouse, use your thumb and two rightmost fingers to move the mouse on your desk. Use your two remaining fingers to press the mouse buttons.

MOUSE ACTIONS

Click

Press and release the left mouse button.

Double-click

Quickly press and release the left mouse button twice.

Right-click

Press and release the right mouse button.

Drag

Position the mouse pointer over an object on your screen and then press and hold down the left mouse button as you move the mouse to where you want to place the object. Then release the button.

START WINDOWS

Windows automatically starts when you turn on your computer. You can immediately perform tasks in Windows.

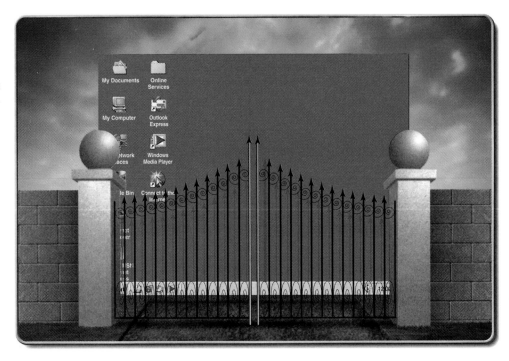

START WINDOWS

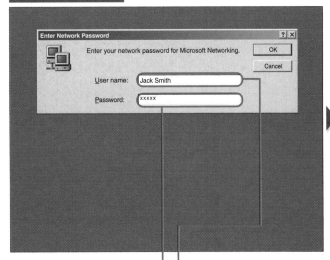

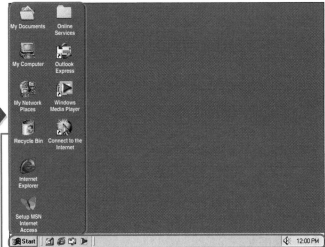

1 Turn on your computer and monitor.

■ A dialog box may appear, asking you to enter your password.

■ This area displays your user name.

2 Type your password and then press the **Enter** key.

Note: A symbol (x) appears for each character you type to prevent others from seeing your password.

■ Windows starts.

■ This area displays your desktop icons.

■ This area displays the taskbar.

Note: The screen resolution in this book was changed to make the information on the screen larger and easier to view. To change the screen resolution, see page 104.

8

SHUT DOWN WINDOWS

When you finish using your computer, you should shut down Windows before turning off the computer.

■ Do not turn off your computer until this message appears on your screen. Some computers will turn off automatically.

Before shutting down Windows, make sure you close all programs you have open.

SHUT DOWN WINDOWS

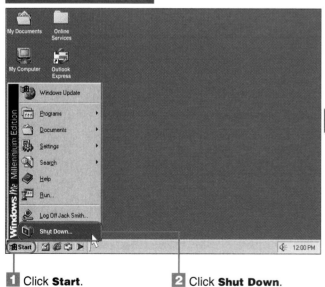

1 Click **Start**.

2 Click **Shut Down**.

■ The Shut Down Windows dialog box appears.

3 Click this area to specify that you want to shut down Windows.

4 Click **Shut down**.

5 Click **OK** to shut down Windows.

USING THE START MENU

You can use the Start menu to access programs, files, computer settings and help with Windows.

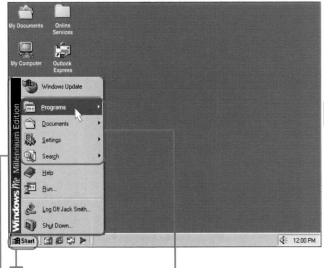

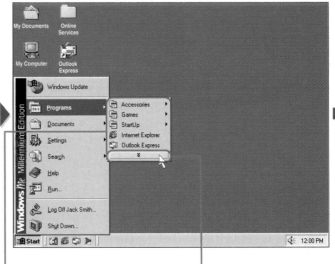

1 Click **Start** to display the Start menu.

■ The Start menu appears.

■ A menu item with an arrow (▶) will display another menu.

2 To display another menu, position the mouse ▷ over the menu item with an arrow (▶).

■ Another menu appears.

■ Windows may display a short version of the menu, which only displays the items you have recently used.

3 To display all the items on the menu, click ⌄.

Which programs does Windows provide?

Windows comes with many useful programs. Here are some examples.

Windows Media Player is a program that allows you to organize and play sound an video files on your computer.

ScanDisk is a program that searches for and repairs hard disk errors.

WordPad is a word processing program that allows you to create simple documents, such as letters and memos.

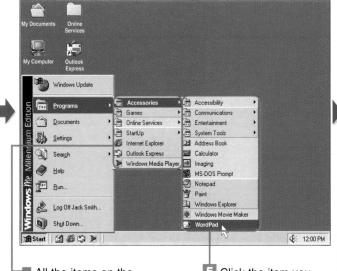

■ All the items on the menu appear.

4 You can repeat steps **2** and **3** until the item you want appears.

5 Click the item you want to use.

Note: To close the Start menu without selecting an item, click outside the menu area or press the **Alt** *key.*

■ In this example, the WordPad window appears.

■ A button for the open window appears on the taskbar.

6 When you finish working with the window, click **X** to close the window.

SCROLL THROUGH A WINDOW

You can use a scroll bar to browse through the information in a window. Scrolling is useful when a window is not large enough to display all the information it contains.

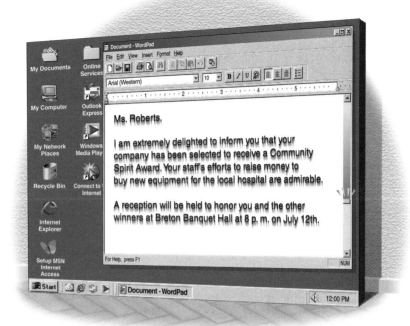

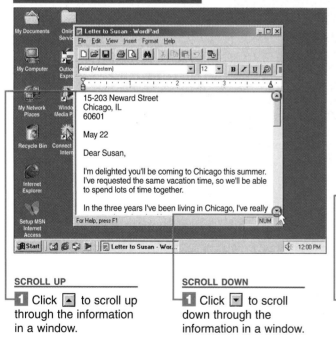

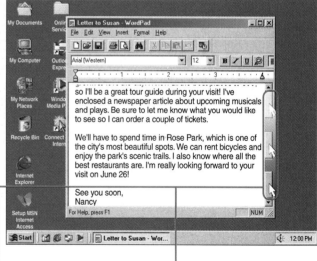

SCROLL UP

1 Click ▲ to scroll up through the information in a window.

SCROLL DOWN

1 Click ▼ to scroll down through the information in a window.

SCROLL TO ANY POSITION

1 Drag the scroll box along the scroll bar until the information you want to view appears.

■ The location of the scroll box indicates which part of the window you are viewing. For example, when the scroll box is halfway down the scroll bar, you are viewing information from the middle of the window.

CLOSE A WINDOW

When you finish working
with a window, you can
close the window to
remove it from your
screen.

CLOSE A WINDOW

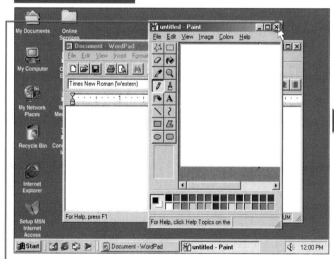

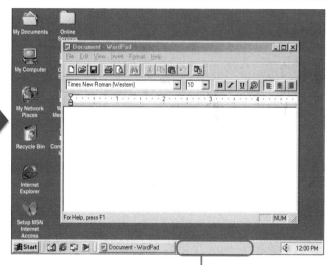

1 Click ⊠ in the window
you want to close.

■ The window disappears
from your screen.

■ The button for the
window disappears
from the taskbar.

MAXIMIZE A WINDOW

You can enlarge a window to fill your entire screen. This allows you to view more of the window's contents.

MAXIMIZE A WINDOW

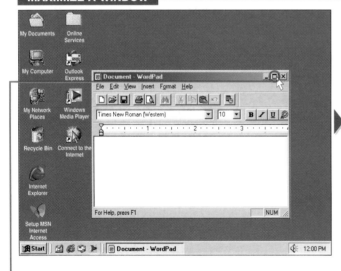

1 Click ▣ in the window you want to maximize.

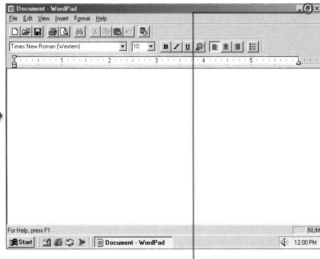

■ The window fills your entire screen.

■ To return the window to its previous size, click ▣ .

14

MINIMIZE A WINDOW

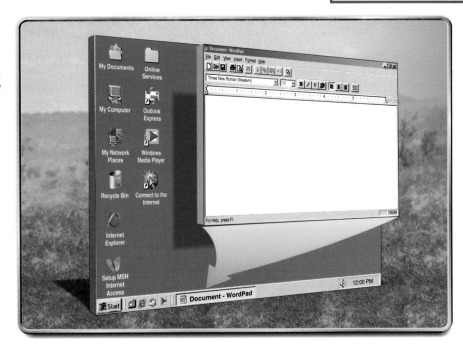

If you are not using a window, you can minimize the window to temporarily remove it from your screen. You can redisplay the window at any time.

MINIMIZE A WINDOW

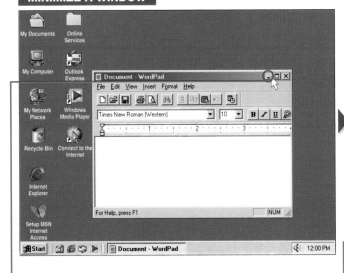

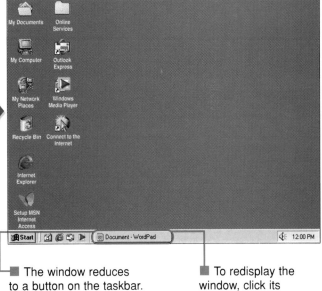

1 Click ▬ in the window you want to minimize.

■ The window reduces to a button on the taskbar.

■ To redisplay the window, click its button on the taskbar.

MOVE A WINDOW

If a window covers items on your screen, you can move the window to a different location.

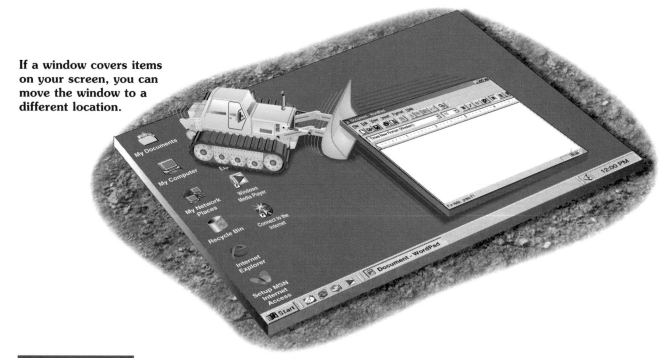

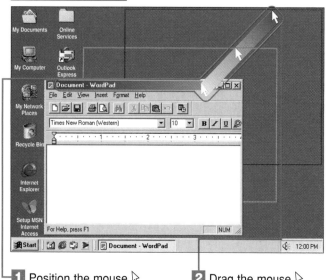

1 Position the mouse over the title bar of the window you want to move.

2 Drag the mouse to where you want to place the window.

■ An outline indicates the new location of the window.

■ The window moves to the new location.

RESIZE A WINDOW

You can easily change the size of a window displayed on your screen.

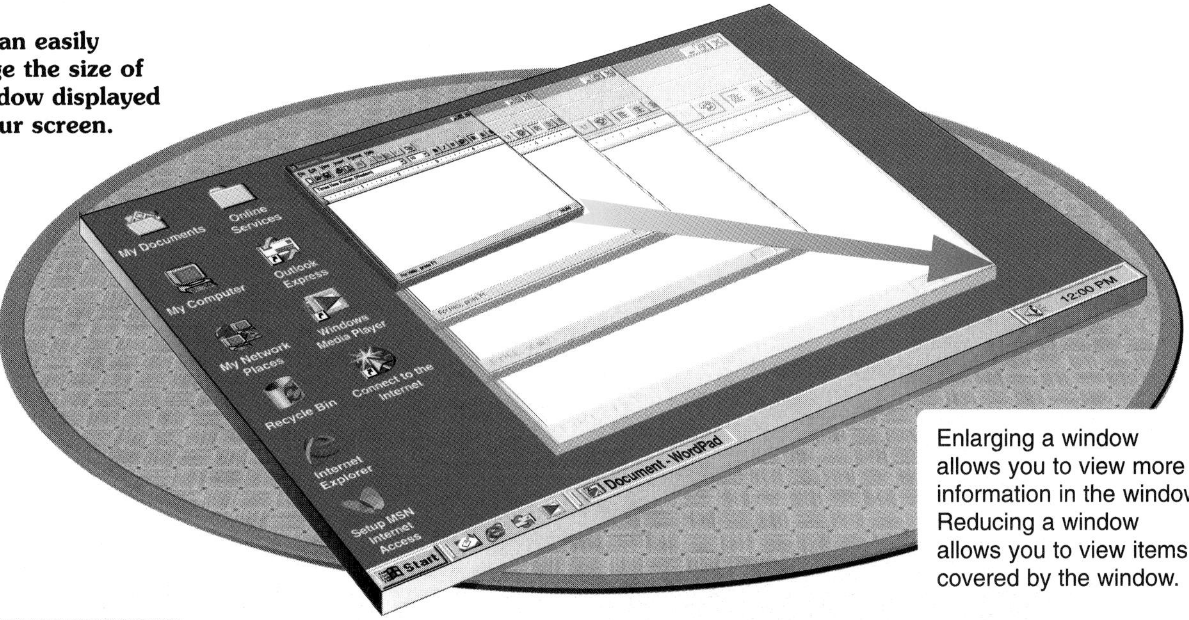

Enlarging a window allows you to view more information in the window. Reducing a window allows you to view items covered by the window.

RESIZE A WINDOW

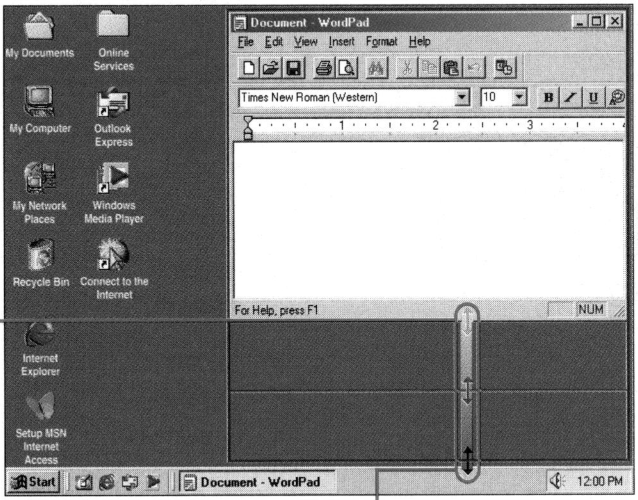

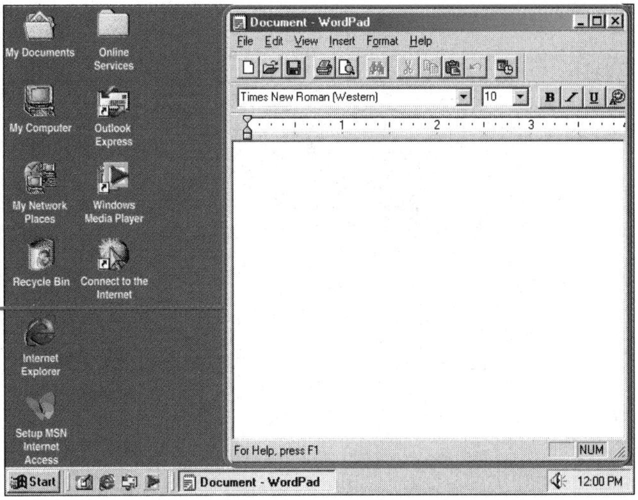

1 Position the mouse ↖ over an edge of the window you want to resize (↖ changes to ↕, ↔ or ⤡).

2 Drag the mouse ↕ until the window displays the size you want.

■ An outline indicates the new size of the window.

■ The window displays the new size.

SWITCH BETWEEN WINDOWS

If you have more than one window open on your screen, you can easily switch between the windows.

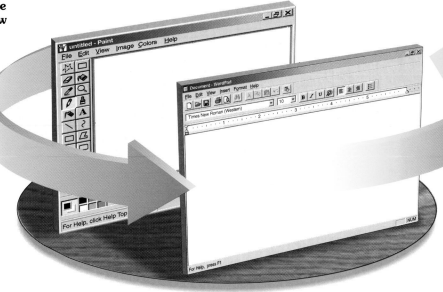

Each window is like a separate piece of paper. Switching between windows allows you to place a different piece of paper at the top of the pile.

SWITCH BETWEEN WINDOWS

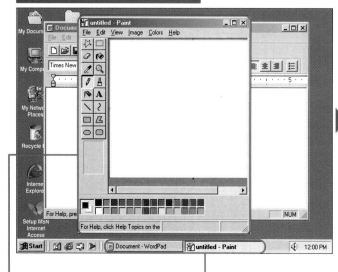

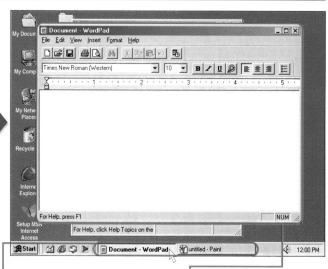

■ You can work in only one window at a time. The active window appears in front of all other windows and displays a blue title bar.

■ The taskbar displays a button for each open window on your screen.

1 To display the window you want to work with in front of all other windows, click its button on the taskbar.

■ The window appears in front of all other windows. You can now clearly view the contents of the window.

Note: You can also display a window in front of all other windows by clicking anywhere inside the window.

SHOW THE DESKTOP

You can instantly minimize all your open windows to remove them from your screen. This allows you to clearly view the desktop.

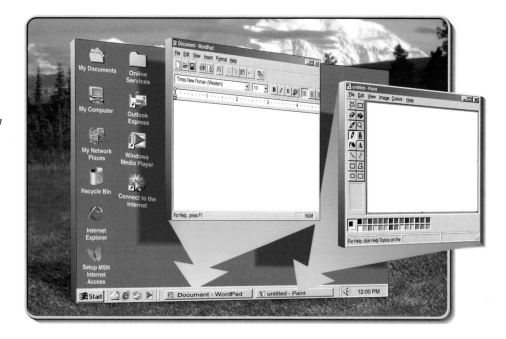

SHOW THE DESKTOP

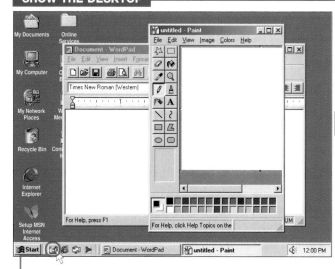

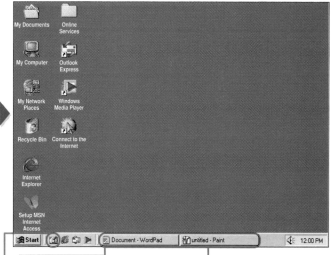

1 Click 📖 to minimize all the open windows on your screen.

■ Each window minimizes to a button on the taskbar. You can now clearly view the desktop.

■ You can click 📖 again to redisplay all the windows.

■ To redisplay only one window, click its button on the taskbar.

19

CLOSE A MISBEHAVING PROGRAM

You can close a program that is no longer responding without having to shut down Windows.

When you close a misbehaving program, you will lose any information you did not save in the program.

CLOSE A MISBEHAVING PROGRAM

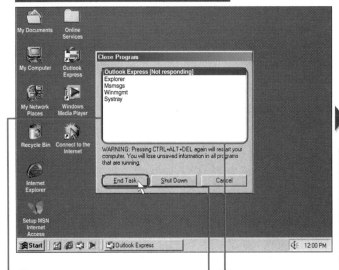

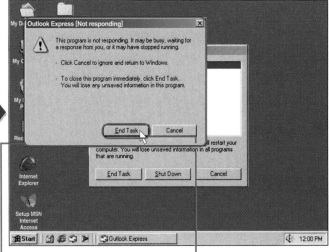

1 To close a misbehaving program, press and hold down the `Ctrl` and `Alt` keys as you press the `Delete` key.

■ The Close Program dialog box appears.

■ This area lists the programs that are currently running.

2 Click the program that is misbehaving.

Note: The phrase [Not responding] appears beside the name of a misbehaving program.

3 Click **End Task**.

■ A dialog box appears, stating that the program is not responding.

4 Click **End Task** to close the program.

RESTART YOUR COMPUTER

If your computer is not operating properly, you can restart your computer to try to fix the problem.

Before restarting your computer, make sure you close all programs you have open.

RESTART YOUR COMPUTER

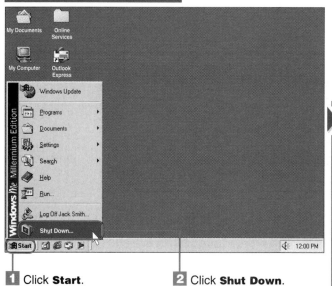

1 Click **Start**.

2 Click **Shut Down**.

■ The Shut Down Windows dialog box appears.

3 Click this area to specify that you want to restart your computer.

4 Click **Restart**.

5 Click **OK** to restart your computer.

21

USING THE CALCULATOR

Windows provides a calculator that you can use to perform calculations.

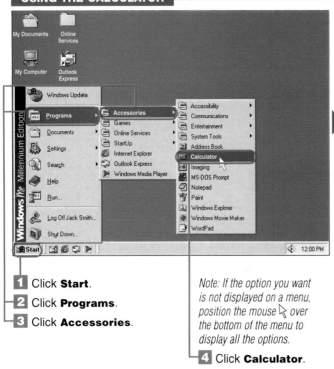

1 Click **Start**.

2 Click **Programs**.

3 Click **Accessories**.

Note: If the option you want is not displayed on a menu, position the mouse ⬉ over the bottom of the menu to display all the options.

4 Click **Calculator**.

■ The Calculator window appears.

5 To enter information into the Calculator, click each button as you would press the buttons on a handheld calculator.

■ This area displays the numbers you enter and the result of each calculation.

■ You can click [C] to start a new calculation at any time.

22

Can I enter numbers using the keys on the right side of my keyboard?

To use the number keys on the right side of your keyboard to enter information into the Calculator, the Num Lock light must be on. To turn the light on, press the `Num Lock` key on your keyboard.

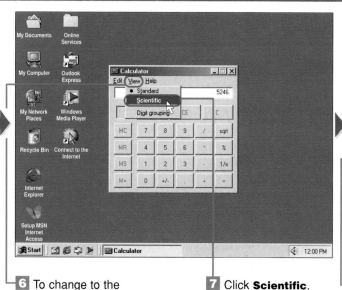

6 To change to the Scientific view of the Calculator, click **View**.

7 Click **Scientific**.

■ The Scientific view of the Calculator appears. This view offers additional features that allow you to perform advanced scientific and statistical calculations.

Note: To return to the Standard view, perform steps 6 and 7, selecting Standard in step 7.

8 When you finish using the Calculator, click **⊠** to close the Calculator window.

FIND HELP INFORMATION

If you do not know how to perform a task in Windows, you can use the Help feature to find information on the task.

FIND HELP INFORMATION

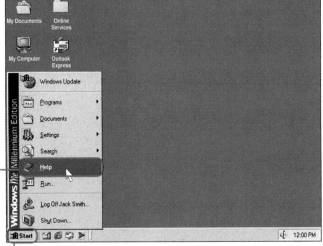

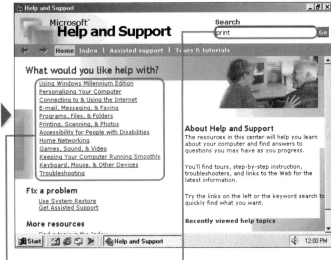

1 Click **Start**.

2 Click **Help**.

■ The Help and Support window appears.

■ This area displays a list of common tasks and problems for which you can receive help.

3 To search for specific help information, click this area and then type a word or short phrase that describes the topic of interest.

4 Press the Enter key to start the search.

**What other ways can I use the
Help feature to find information?**

Assisted support

Allows you to find
help information
on the Internet.

Home

Allows you to browse through
common tasks and problems
by category to find help
information. The Home page
appears each time you open
the Help and Support window.

Index

Provides an alphabetical
list of help topics that
offer help information.

Tours & tutorials

Provides tours and
tutorials that offer
information about
Windows.

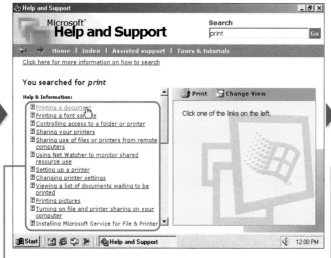

■ This area displays
help topics that match the
information you entered.

5 Click the help topic of
interest (⍓ changes to 🖑
when over a help topic).

*Note: Most topics with the 📄
symbol require a connection
to the Internet. Topics with the
❓ symbol do not require a
connection to the Internet.*

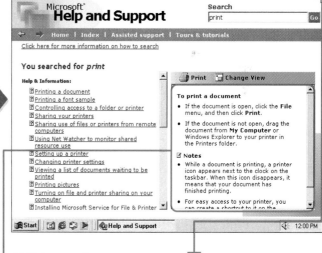

■ This area displays
information for the help
topic you selected.

*Note: You can repeat step 5 to
display information for another
help topic.*

6 When you finish
reviewing help information,
click ⊠ to close the Help
and Support window.

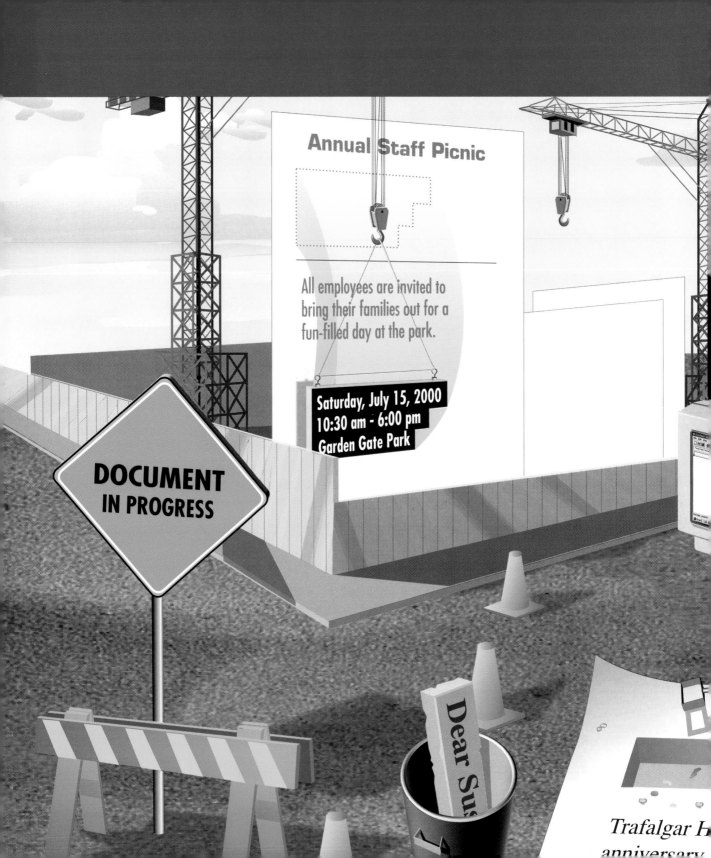

CHAPTER 2

Create Documents

In this chapter you will learn how to create and edit documents quickly and efficiently using the WordPad program.

*chool celebrates its 30*th

START WORDPAD

You can use WordPad to create simple documents, such as letters and memos.

START WORDPAD

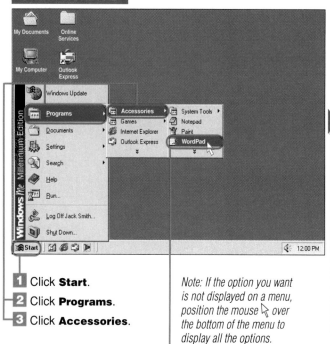

1 Click **Start**.

2 Click **Programs**.

3 Click **Accessories**.

Note: If the option you want is not displayed on a menu, position the mouse ⌖ over the bottom of the menu to display all the options.

4 Click **WordPad**.

■ The WordPad window appears, displaying a blank document.

■ The flashing line on your screen, called the insertion point, indicates where the text you type will appear.

5 Click 🗖 to enlarge the WordPad window to fill your screen.

Are there more sophisticated programs that I can use to create documents?

WordPad is a simple program that offers only basic word processing features. If you need more advanced features, you can purchase a more powerful word processor, such as Microsoft Word or Corel WordPerfect. These programs include features such as tables, graphics, a spell checker and a thesaurus.

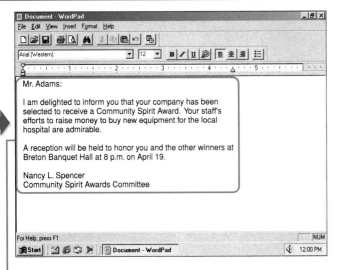

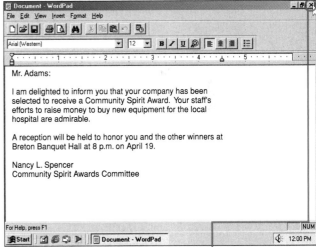

6 Type the text for your document.

■ When you reach the end of a line, WordPad automatically moves the text to the next line. You need to press the `Enter` key only when you want to start a new line or paragraph.

Note: In this example, the font and size of text was changed to make the text easier to read. To change the font and size of text, see pages 32 and 33.

EXIT WORDPAD

You can exit WordPad when you finish using the program.

■ Before exiting WordPad, make sure you save any changes you made to the document. To save your changes, see page 34.

1 Click ☒ to exit WordPad.

EDIT TEXT

You can easily edit the text in your document. You can remove text you no longer need as well as add new text to the document.

EDIT TEXT

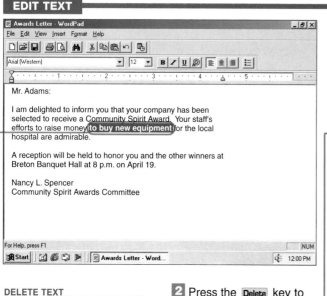

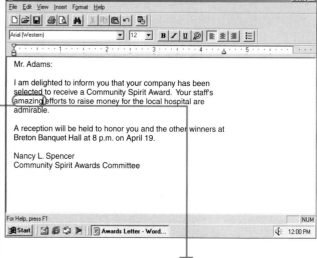

DELETE TEXT

■1 To select the text you want to delete, drag the mouse I over the text until the text is highlighted.

■2 Press the Delete key to remove the text.

■ To delete one character at a time, click to the left of the first character you want to delete. Press the Delete key for each character you want to remove.

INSERT TEXT

■1 Click the location where you want to insert text.

■ The flashing insertion point indicates where the text you type will appear.

■2 Type the text you want to insert.

■3 To insert a blank space, press the **Spacebar**.

BOLD, ITALICIZE OR UNDERLINE TEXT

You can bold, italicize or underline text to emphasize information in your document.

BOLD, ITALICIZE OR UNDERLINE TEXT

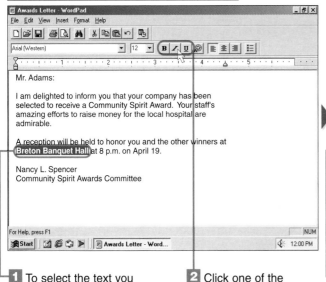

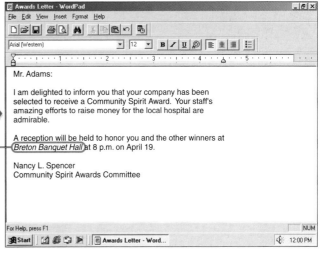

1 To select the text you want to change to a new style, drag the mouse I over the text until the text is highlighted.

2 Click one of the following options.

B Bold

I Italic

<u>U</u> Underline

■ The text you selected appears in the new style.

■ To deselect text, click outside the selected area.

■ To remove a bold, italic or underline style, repeat steps **1** and **2**.

CHANGE FONT OF TEXT

You can enhance the appearance of your document by changing the design of the text.

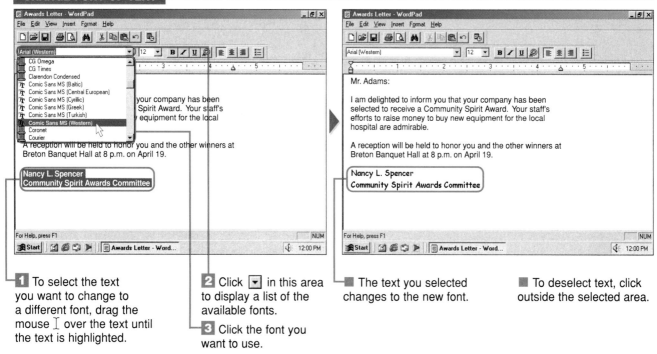

1 To select the text you want to change to a different font, drag the mouse I over the text until the text is highlighted.

2 Click ▼ in this area to display a list of the available fonts.

3 Click the font you want to use.

■ The text you selected changes to the new font.

■ To deselect text, click outside the selected area.

32

**You can increase
or decrease the
size of text in
your document.**

Larger text is
easier to read,
but smaller text
allows you to fit
more information
on a page.

CHANGE SIZE OF TEXT

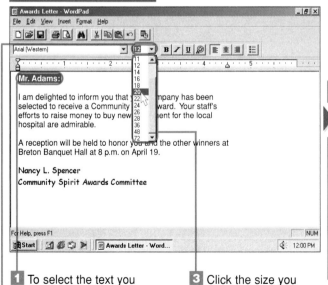

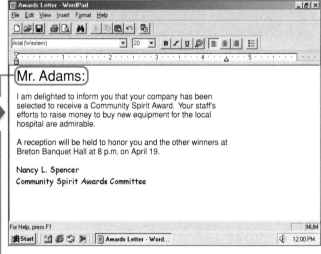

1 To select the text you
want to change to a new
size, drag the mouse I
over the text until the text
is highlighted.

2 Click ▼ in this area
to display a list of the
available sizes.

3 Click the size you
want to use.

*Note: WordPad measures the
size of text in points. There
are approximately 72 points
in one inch.*

■ The text you selected
changes to the new size.

■ To deselect text, click
outside the selected area.

33

SAVE A DOCUMENT

You should save your document to store it for future use. This allows you to later review and edit the document.

You should regularly save changes you make to a document to avoid losing your work.

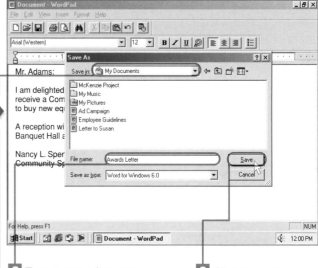

1 Click 🖫 to save your document.

■ The Save As dialog box appears.

Note: If you previously saved your document, the Save As dialog box will not appear since you have already named the document.

2 Type a name for your document.

■ This area shows the location where WordPad will store your document. You can click this area to change the location.

3 Click **Save** to save your document.

34

You can open a
saved document
to display the
document on
your screen.
This allows you
to review and
make changes
to the document.

WordPad allows you
to work with only one
document at a time. If you
are currently working with
a document, make sure
you save the document
before opening another
document. To save a
document, see page 34.

OPEN A DOCUMENT

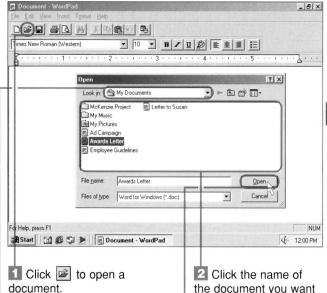

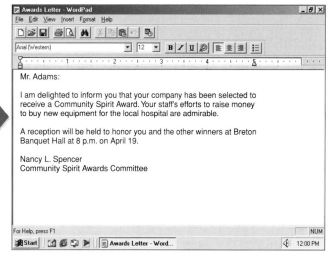

1 Click 🖼 to open a
document.

■ The Open dialog box
appears.

■ This area shows the
location of the displayed
documents. You can click this
area to change the location.

2 Click the name of
the document you want
to open.

3 Click **Open** to open
the document.

■ The document opens and
appears on your screen. You
can now review and make
changes to the document.

CHAPTER 3

Create Pictures

Learn how to create, erase and save your own pictures using the Paint program.

START PAINT

You can use Paint to draw pictures on your computer.

You can place the pictures you draw in Paint in other programs. For example, you can add your company logo to a business letter you created in WordPad.

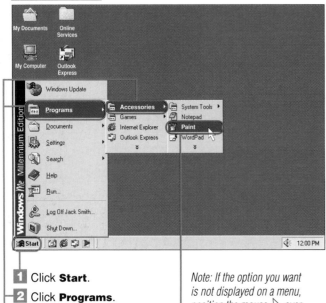

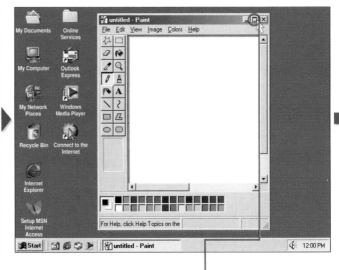

1 Click **Start**.

2 Click **Programs**.

3 Click **Accessories**.

Note: If the option you want is not displayed on a menu, position the mouse ⌖ over the bottom of the menu to display all the options.

4 Click **Paint**.

■ The Paint window appears.

5 Click ☐ to enlarge the Paint window to fill your screen.

Are there more sophisticated programs that I can use to draw pictures on my computer?

Paint is a simple program that offers basic features to help you create pictures. You may want to obtain a more sophisticated image editing program that offers more advanced features, such as Paint Shop Pro or Adobe Photoshop. You can obtain Paint Shop Pro at the www.jasc.com Web site and Adobe Photoshop at the www.adobe.com Web site.

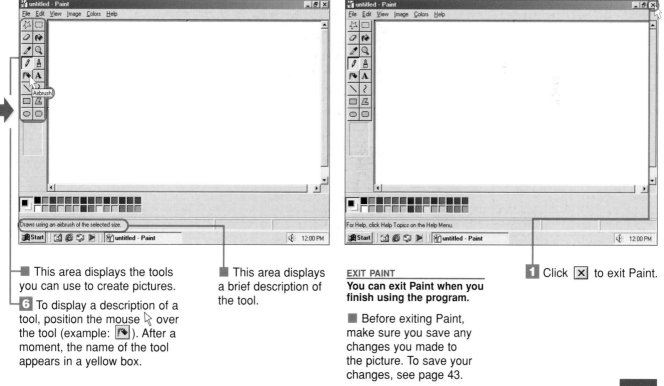

■ This area displays the tools you can use to create pictures.

6 To display a description of a tool, position the mouse ↘ over the tool (example: 🖰). After a moment, the name of the tool appears in a yellow box.

■ This area displays a brief description of the tool.

EXIT PAINT

You can exit Paint when you finish using the program.

■ Before exiting Paint, make sure you save any changes you made to the picture. To save your changes, see page 43.

1 Click ✕ to exit Paint.

DRAW SHAPES

You can draw shapes such as circles, squares and polygons in various colors.

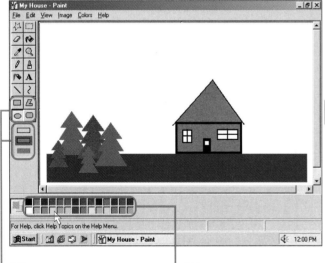

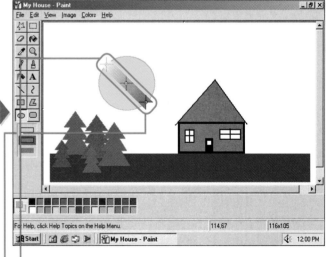

1 Click the tool for the type of shape you want to draw.

2 Click an option to specify if you want the shape to display an outline, an inside color or both.

3 To select a color for the outline of the shape, click the color.

4 To select a color for the inside of the shape, right-click the color.

5 Position the mouse ⟋ where you want to begin drawing the shape (⟋ changes to ┼).

6 Drag the mouse ┼ until the shape is the size you want.

■ If you selected ▨ in step **1**, repeat steps **5** and **6** until you finish drawing all the lines for the shape. Then immediately double-click the mouse to complete the shape.

DRAW LINES

You can draw straight, wavy and curved lines in various colors.

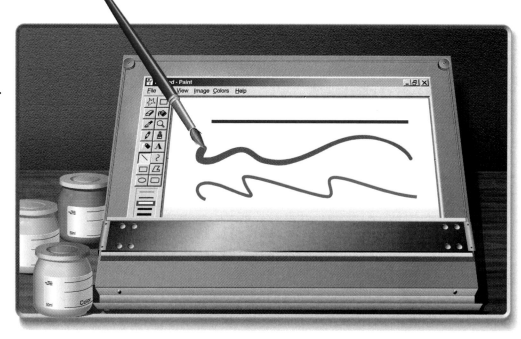

DRAW LINES

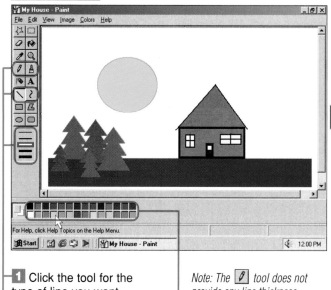

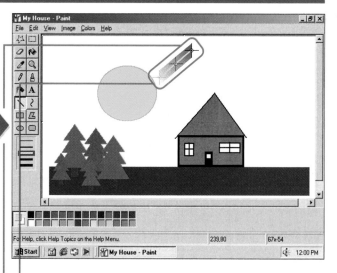

1 Click the tool for the type of line you want to draw.

2 To select a line thickness, click one of the options in this area.

Note: The ✐ *tool does not provide any line thickness options.*

3 To select a color for the line, click the color.

4 Position the mouse ⬚ where you want to begin drawing the line (⬚ changes to ┼, ✐ or ┼).

5 Drag the mouse ┼ until the line is the length you want.

■ If you selected 〜 in step **1**, position the mouse ┼ over the line and then drag the mouse until the line curves the way you want. Then immediately click the mouse to complete the curved line.

41

ERASE PART OF A PICTURE

You can use the Eraser tool to remove part of your picture.

ERASE PART OF A PICTURE

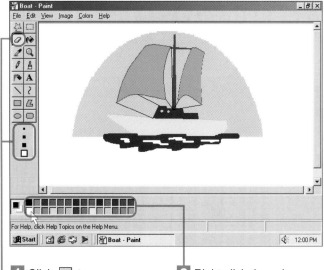

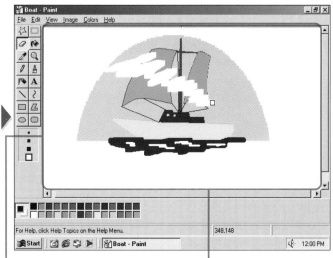

1 Click ✏ to erase part of your picture.

2 Click the size of eraser you want to use.

3 Right-click the color you want to use for the eraser (example: ☐).

Note: Make sure you select a color that matches the background color of your picture.

4 Position the mouse ⬉ where you want to begin erasing (⬉ changes to ☐).

5 Drag the mouse ☐ over the area you want to erase.

Note: To immediately undo the change, press and hold down the **Ctrl** *key as you press the* **Z** *key.*

42

SAVE A PICTURE

You should save
your picture to
store the picture
for future use.
This allows you
to later review
and make changes
to the picture.

You should regularly
save changes you
make to a picture
to avoid losing your
work.

SAVE A PICTURE

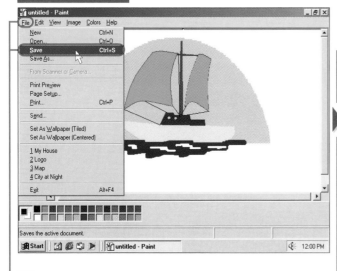

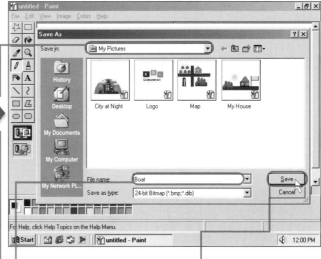

1 Click **File**.

2 Click **Save**.

■ The Save As dialog
box appears.

*Note: If you previously saved
the picture, the Save As dialog
box will not appear since you
have already named the picture.*

3 Type a name for your
picture.

■ This area shows the
location where Paint will
store the picture. You can
click this area to change
the location.

4 Click **Save** to save
your picture.

OPEN A PICTURE

You can open a
saved picture to
display the picture
on your screen. This
allows you to review
and make changes
to the picture.

OPEN A PICTURE

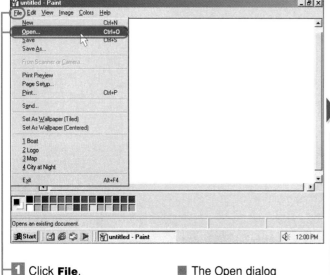

■1 Click **File**.

■2 Click **Open**.

■ The Open dialog
box appears.

■ By default, Windows displays
the pictures stored in the My
Pictures folder. You can click
this area to change the location
of the displayed pictures.

■ This area shows a miniature
version of each picture stored
in the My Pictures folder.

■3 Click the picture
you want to open.

■4 Click **Open** to
open the picture.

Can I work with two pictures at the same time?

Paint allows you to work with only one picture at a time. If you are currently working with a picture, make sure you save the picture before opening another picture. To save a picture, see page 43.

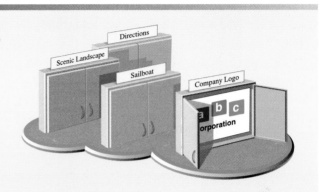

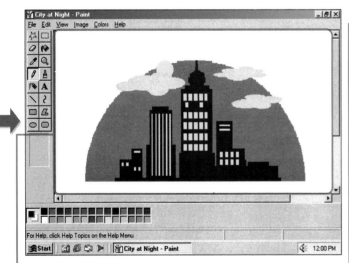

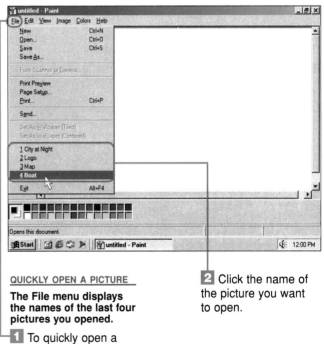

■ The picture opens and appears on your screen. You can now review and make changes to the picture.

QUICKLY OPEN A PICTURE

The File menu displays the names of the last four pictures you opened.

1 To quickly open a picture, click **File**.

2 Click the name of the picture you want to open.

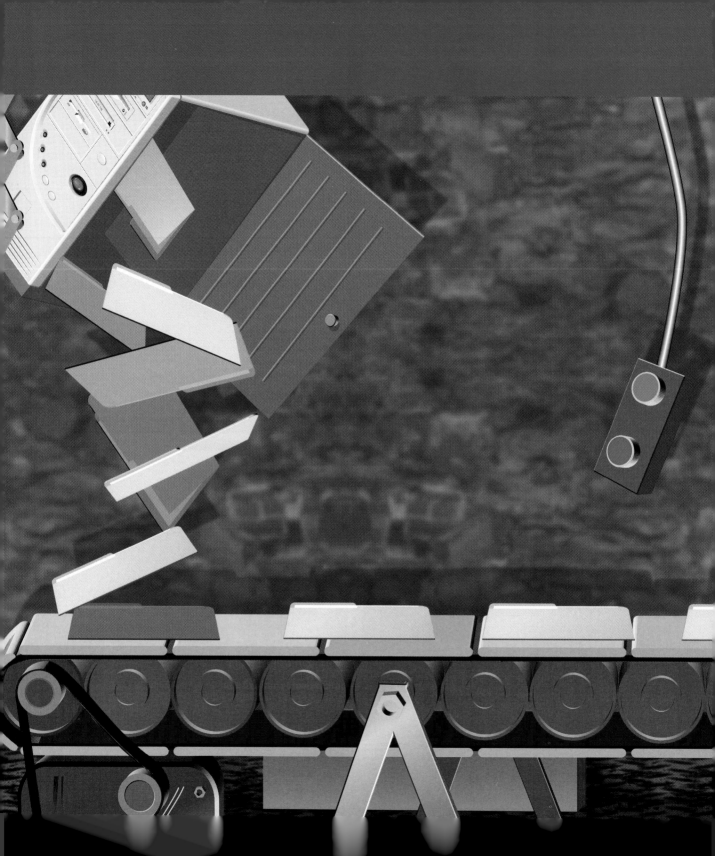

CHAPTER 4

View Files

In this chapter learn how to view and sort your files, folders and programs for easier access.

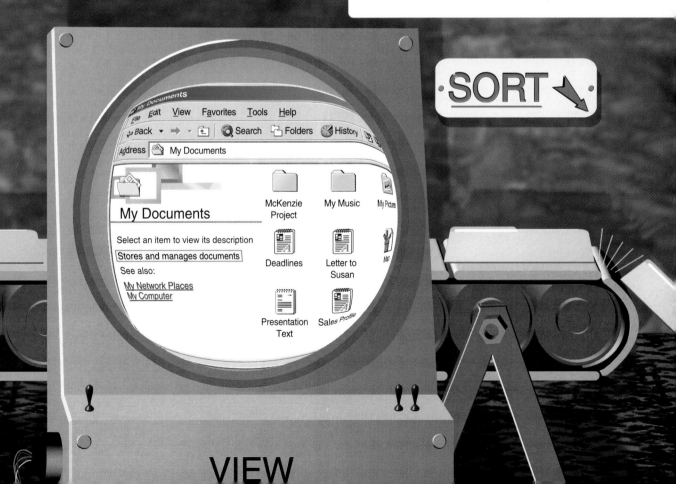

SORT

VIEW

VIEW CONTENTS OF YOUR COMPUTER

You can easily view the drives, folders and files on your computer.

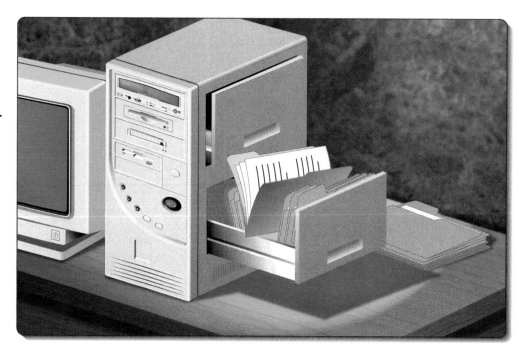

VIEW CONTENTS OF YOUR COMPUTER

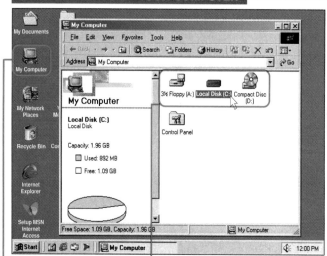

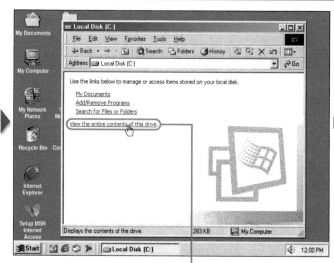

1 Double-click **My Computer** to view the contents of your computer.

■ The My Computer window appears.

■ These items represent the drives on your computer.

2 To display the contents of a drive, double-click the drive.

Note: If you want to view the contents of a floppy or CD-ROM drive, make sure you insert a floppy disk or CD-ROM disc before performing step 2.

■ The contents of the drive appear.

3 If the contents of the drive do not appear, click **View the entire contents of this drive** to display the contents of the drive.

What drives are available on my computer?

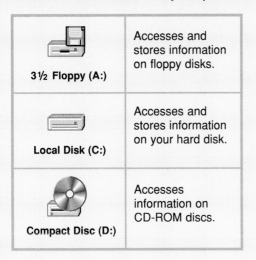 3½ Floppy (A:)	Accesses and stores information on floppy disks.
Local Disk (C:)	Accesses and stores information on your hard disk.
Compact Disc (D:)	Accesses information on CD-ROM discs.

What do the icons in a window represent?

Each item in a window displays an icon to help you distinguish between the different types of items. Common types of items include:

 Folder

 Paint picture

 Text document

 Windows Media Player File

 WordPad document

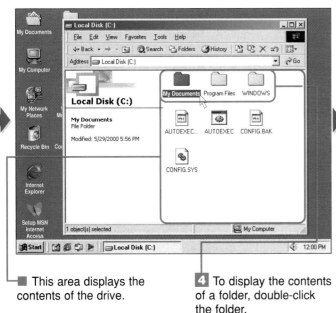

■ This area displays the contents of the drive.

4 To display the contents of a folder, double-click the folder.

■ The contents of the folder appear.

5 To view information about a folder or file, click the item.

■ This area displays information about the item.

Note: If information about the item does not appear, you may need to increase the size of the window. To resize a window, see page 17.

■ You can click **Back** to return to a window you have previously viewed.

49

CHANGE APPEARANCE OF ITEMS

You can change the appearance of items in a window. The appearance you select determines the information you will see in the window.

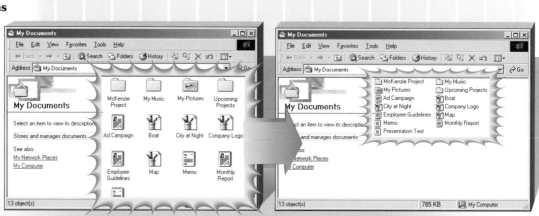

CHANGE APPEARANCE OF ITEMS

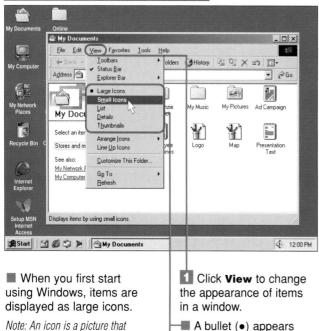

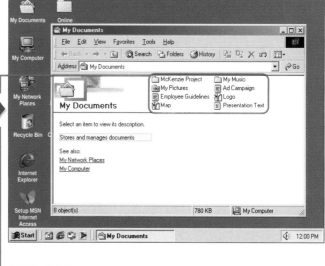

■ When you first start using Windows, items are displayed as large icons.

Note: An icon is a picture that represents an item such as a file, folder or program.

1 Click **View** to change the appearance of items in a window.

■ A bullet (•) appears beside the current view of the items.

2 Click the way you want to display the items.

SMALL ICONS

■ The Small Icons view displays items as small icons.

50

What is the Thumbnails view?

The Thumbnails view allows you to display a miniature version of each image file in a window. Non-image files display an icon to indicate the type of file, such as a folder (🗀) or WordPad document (📄). The Thumbnails view is not available in some windows.

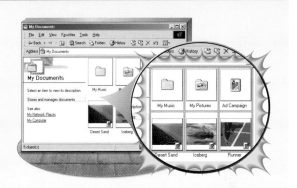

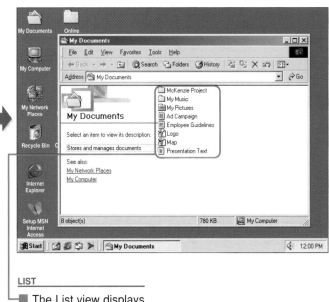

LIST

■ The List view displays items as small icons arranged in a list.

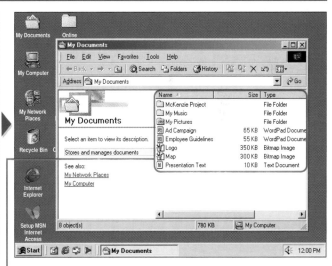

DETAILS

■ The Details view displays information about each item, such as the name, size and type of item.

SORT ITEMS

You can sort the items displayed in a window to help you find files and folders more easily.

You can sort items by name, size, type or the date the items were last changed.

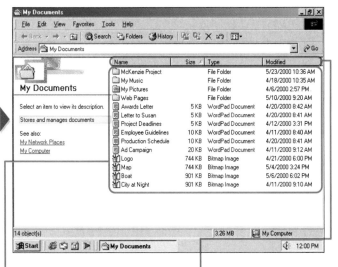

■ When you first start using Windows, items are sorted alphabetically by name.

1 Click the heading for the column you want to use to sort the items.

Note: If the headings are not displayed, perform steps 1 and 2 on page 50, selecting **Details** *in step 2.*

■ The items are sorted. In this example, the items are sorted by size.

■ To sort the items in the reverse order, click the heading again.

VIEW CONTENTS OF MY DOCUMENTS FOLDER

You can easily view the contents of the My Documents folder. This folder provides a convenient place to store your files.

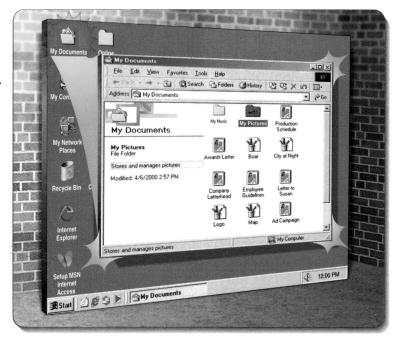

Many programs automatically store files you save in the My Documents folder.

VIEW CONTENTS OF MY DOCUMENTS FOLDER

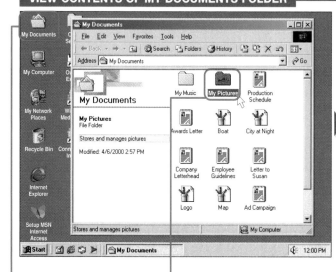

1 Double-click My Documents.

■ The My Documents window appears, displaying your files and folders.

■ The My Pictures folder provides a convenient place to store your images.

2 To display the contents of the My Pictures folder, double-click the folder.

■ The My Pictures window appears, displaying a miniature version of each image in the My Pictures folder.

3 When you finish viewing the images, click ☒ to close the window.

USING WINDOWS EXPLORER

Windows Explorer shows the location of every folder and file on your computer.

You can move, rename and delete files in the Windows Explorer window as you would in any window. To work with files, see pages 58 to 87.

USING WINDOWS EXPLORER

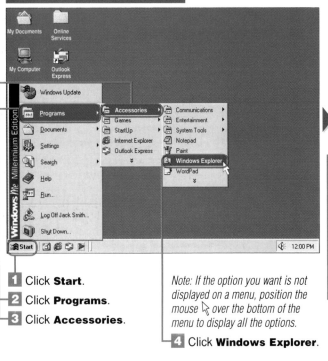

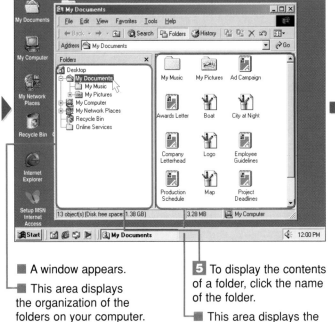

1 Click **Start**.

2 Click **Programs**.

3 Click **Accessories**.

Note: If the option you want is not displayed on a menu, position the mouse ↳ over the bottom of the menu to display all the options.

4 Click **Windows Explorer**.

■ A window appears.

■ This area displays the organization of the folders on your computer.

5 To display the contents of a folder, click the name of the folder.

■ This area displays the contents of the folder.

How can I tell if a folder contains other folders?

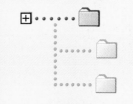

A plus sign (⊞) beside a folder indicates that all the folders it contains are hidden.

A minus sign (⊟) beside a folder indicates that all the folders it contains are displayed.

No sign beside a folder indicates that the folder does not contain any folders, although it may contain files.

■ A folder displaying a plus sign (⊞) contains hidden folders.

6 Click the plus sign (⊞) beside the folder to display its hidden folders.

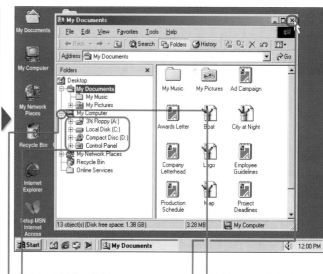

■ The hidden folders appear.

■ The plus sign (⊞) beside the folder changes to a minus sign (⊟). This indicates that all the folders within the folder are displayed.

■ You can click the minus sign (⊟) to once again hide the folders within the folder.

7 When you finish using Windows Explorer, click ☒ to close the window.

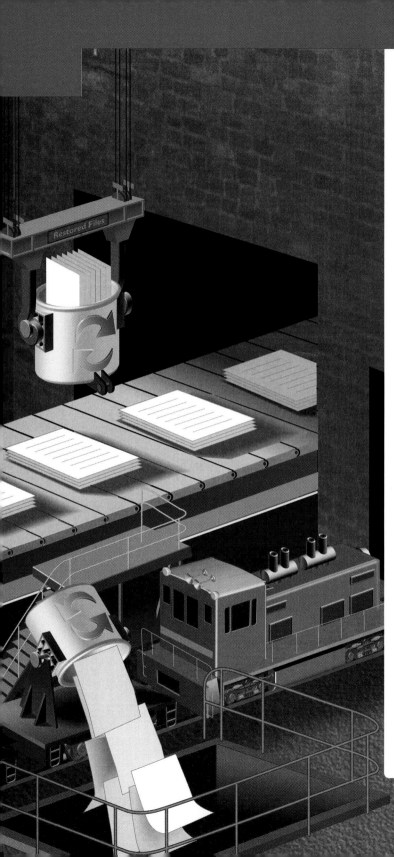

CHAPTER 5

Work with Files

This chapter will show you how to open, print and copy files. You will also learn how to create shortcuts, empty the Recycle Bin and search for files on your computer.

SELECT FILES

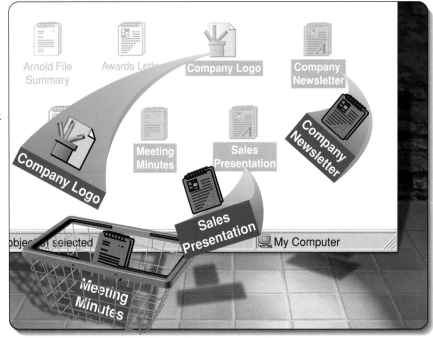

Before working with files, you often need to select the files you want to work with. Selected files appear highlighted on your screen.

You can select folders the same way you select files. Selecting a folder will select all the files in the folder.

SELECT FILES

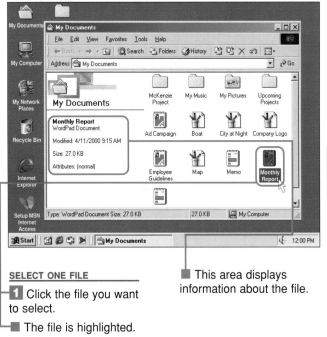

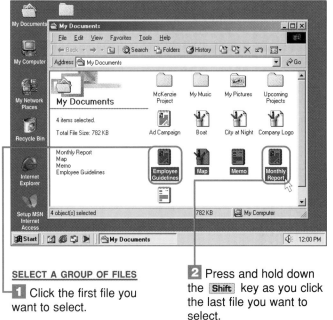

SELECT ONE FILE

1 Click the file you want to select.

■ The file is highlighted.

■ This area displays information about the file.

SELECT A GROUP OF FILES

1 Click the first file you want to select.

2 Press and hold down the `Shift` key as you click the last file you want to select.

How do I deselect files?

To deselect all the files in a window, click a blank area in the window.

To deselect one file from a group of selected files, press and hold down the `Ctrl` key as you click the file you want to deselect.

Note: You can deselect folders the same way you deselect files.

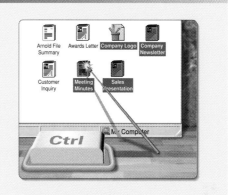

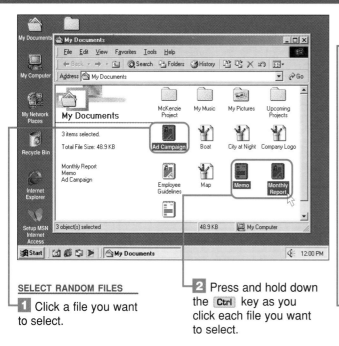

SELECT RANDOM FILES

1 Click a file you want to select.

2 Press and hold down the `Ctrl` key as you click each file you want to select.

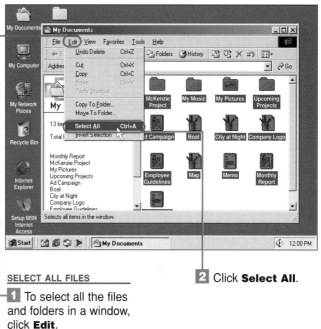

SELECT ALL FILES

1 To select all the files and folders in a window, click **Edit**.

2 Click **Select All**.

OPEN A FILE

You can open a
file to display its
contents on your
screen. This allows
you to review and
make changes to
the file.

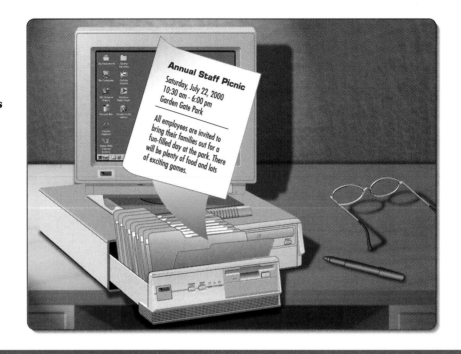

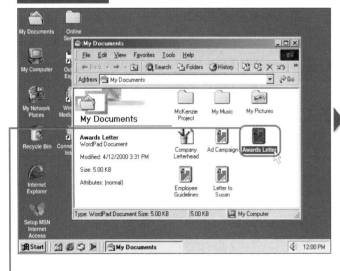

1 Double-click the
file you want to open.

■ The file opens. You can
review and make changes
to the file.

*Note: If you opened an image file,
the image will appear in the Image
Preview window. To edit the image,
you need to open the image within the
program you used to create the image
or in any image editing program.*

2 When you finish
working with the file,
click ✗ to close
the file.

Windows keeps track
of the files you most
recently used. You
can quickly open any
of these files.

OPEN A RECENTLY USED FILE

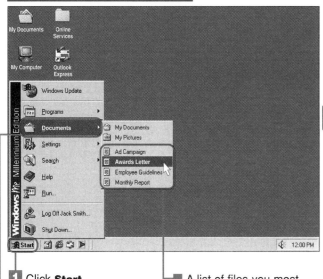

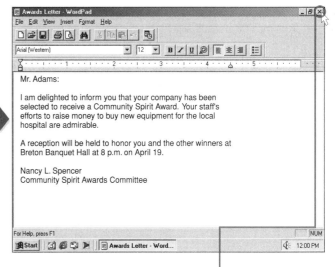

1 Click **Start**.

2 Click **Documents**.

■ A list of files you most
recently used appears.

3 Click the file you want
to open.

*Note: You can click **My Documents**
or **My Pictures** to open folders that
store documents or images.*

■ The file opens. You can
review and make changes
to the file.

*Note: If you opened an image file,
the image will appear in the Image
Preview window. To edit the image,
you need to open the image within the
program you used to create the image
or in any image editing program.*

4 When you finish
working with the file,
click ✕ to close
the file.

PRINT A FILE

You can produce a paper copy of a file stored on your computer.

Before printing a file, make sure your printer is turned on and contains paper.

PRINT A FILE

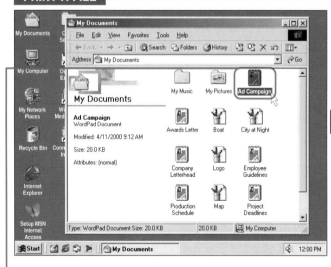

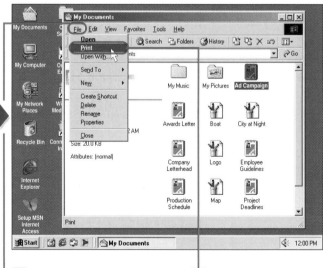

1 Click the file you want to print.

■ To print more than one file, select all of the files you want to print.

Note: To select multiple files, see page 58.

2 Click **File**.

3 Click **Print**.

What types of printers can I use to print my files?

Windows works with many types of printers. There are two common types of printers.

Ink-jet

An ink-jet printer produces documents that are suitable for routine business and personal use.

Laser

A laser printer is faster and produces higher-quality documents than an ink-jet printer, but is more expensive.

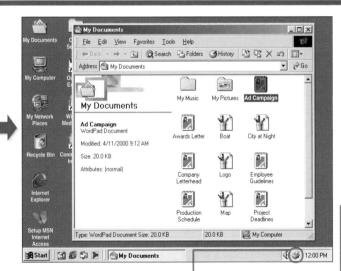

■ Windows quickly opens, prints and then closes the file.

■ When you print a file, a printer icon (🖨) appears in this area. The icon disappears when the file has finished printing.

PRINT A FILE LOCATED ON THE DESKTOP

1 Right-click the file you want to print. A menu appears.

2 Click **Print** to print the file.

■ Windows quickly opens, prints and then closes the file.

VIEW FILES SENT TO THE PRINTER

You can view information about the files you have sent to the printer.

VIEW FILES SENT TO THE PRINTER

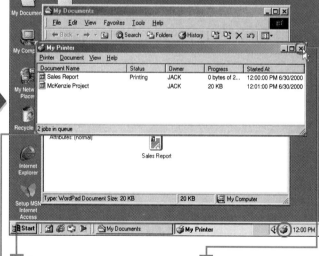

■ When you print a file, the printer icon (🖨) appears in this area.

■ A yellow box appears, displaying the number of files.

1 To see how many files are waiting to print, position the mouse over the printer icon (🖨).

2 Double-click the printer icon (🖨) to view information about the files waiting to print.

■ A window appears, displaying information about the files. The file at the top of the list will print first.

3 When you finish viewing the information, click ✖ to close the window.

You can stop a file
from printing. This
is useful if you want
to make last-minute
changes to the file.

CANCEL PRINTING

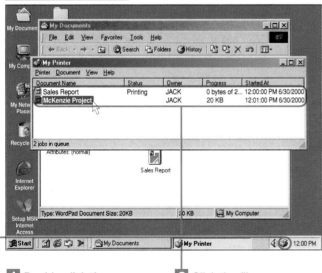

1 Double-click the
printer icon (🖨).

■ A window appears,
displaying information
about the files waiting
to print.

2 Click the file you
no longer want to print.

3 Press the `Delete` key
and the file disappears
from the list.

4 Click ✕ to close
the window.

RENAME A FILE

You can give a
file a new name
to better describe
the contents of the
file. Renaming a
file can make the
file easier to find.

You can rename
folders the same
way you rename
files. You should
only rename
folders that you
have created.

RENAME A FILE

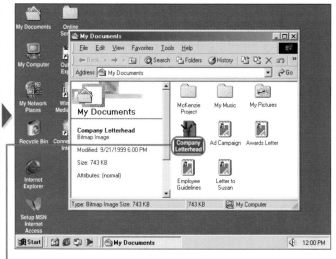

1 Click the name of the
file you want to rename.

*Note: You should only rename
files that you have created.*

2 Wait a moment and
then click the name of
the file again.

■ The name of the file
appears in a box.

3 Type a new name for
the file and then press
the **Enter** key.

*Note: A file name cannot contain
the \ /:*?" < > or | characters.
Try to keep your file names short
since some programs cannot
understand extremely long file
names.*

UNDO LAST CHANGE

If you regret a
change you made
to a file, you can
use the Undo
feature to cancel
the change.

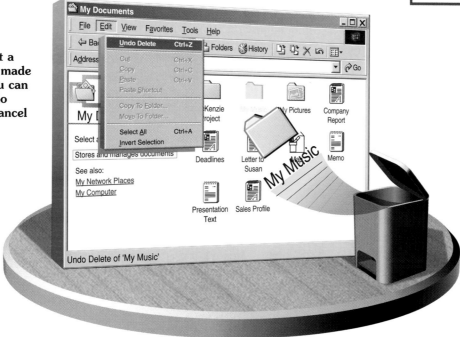

Undo Delete of 'My Music'

Windows can
undo changes
such as renaming,
deleting or moving
a file. You cannot
undo all changes
you make to a file.

UNDO LAST CHANGE

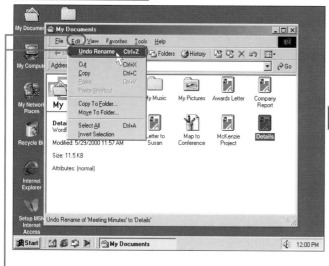

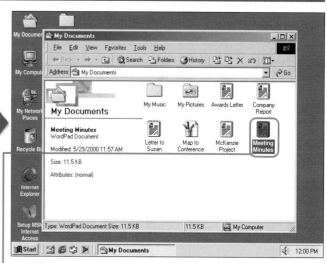

■1 Click **Edit**.

■2 Click **Undo**.

*Note: The word that appears
beside the Undo command
indicates which change
Windows will undo.*

■ Windows cancels the
last change you made.

MOVE AND COPY FILES

You can organize the files stored on your computer by moving or copying them to new locations.

Organizing files on your computer is similar to organizing files in a filing cabinet.

MOVE FILES

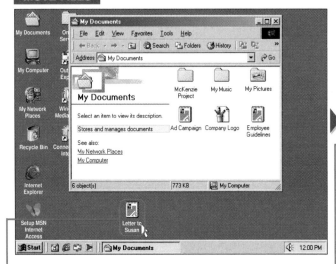

1 Position the mouse ⌖ over the file you want to move.

■ To move more than one file at the same time, select all the files you want to move. Then position the mouse ⌖ over one of the files.

Note: To select more than one file, see page 58.

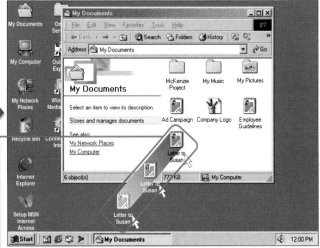

2 Drag the file to a new location on your computer.

What is the difference between moving and copying a file?

Move a File

When you move a file, you place the file in a new location on your computer.

Copy a File

When you copy a file, you make an exact copy of the file and then place the copy in a new location. This lets you store the file in two locations.

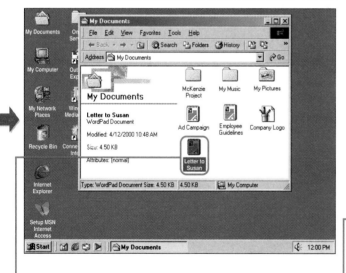

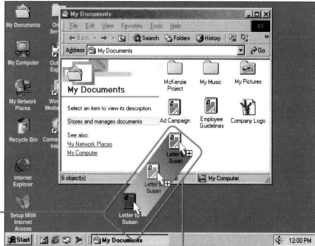

COPY FILES

■ The file moves to the new location.

Note: You can move folders the same way you move files. When you move a folder, all the files in the folder also move.

1 Position the mouse ⇧ over the file you want to copy.

■ To copy more than one file at the same time, select all the files you want to copy. Then position the mouse ⇧ over one of the files.

Note: To select more than one file, see page 58.

2 Press and hold down the **Ctrl** key as you drag the file to a new location.

COPY A FILE TO A FLOPPY DISK

You can copy a file stored on your computer to a floppy disk. This is useful if you want to give a friend, family member or colleague a copy of the file.

When copying a file to a floppy disk, you must use a formatted floppy disk. To format a floppy disk, see page 190.

COPY A FILE TO A FLOPPY DISK

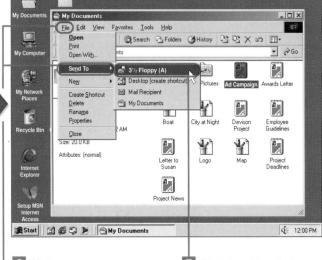

1 Insert a floppy disk into your floppy drive.

2 Click the file you want to copy to a floppy disk.

■ To copy more than one file, select all the files you want to copy.

Note: To select multiple files, see page 58.

3 Click **File**.

4 Click **Send To**.

5 Click the drive that contains the floppy disk.

**How can I protect the information
on my floppy disks?**

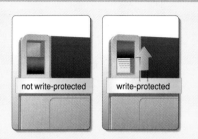

not write-protected   write-protected

Store in a Safe Location

You should keep floppy disks away
from magnets, which can damage
the information stored on the disks.
Also be careful not to spill liquids,
such as coffee or soda, on the disks.

Write-protect

You can prevent other people from
making changes to information on
a floppy disk by sliding the tab on
the disk to the write-protected
position.

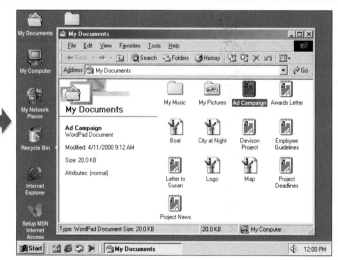

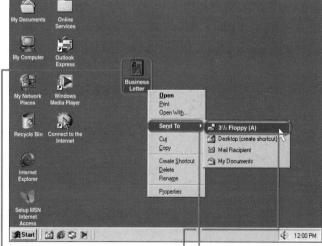

■ Windows places a
copy of the file on the
floppy disk.

*Note: To view the contents of
a floppy disk, see page 48.*

*Note: You can copy a folder to
a floppy disk the same way you
copy a file. When you copy a
folder, Windows copies all the
files in the folder.*

**COPY A FILE ON YOUR
DESKTOP**

■1 Insert a floppy disk
into your floppy drive.

■2 Right-click the file you
want to copy to a floppy
disk. A menu appears.

■3 Click **Send To**.

■4 Click the drive that
contains the floppy disk.

DELETE A FILE

You can delete a file you no longer need.

Before you delete a file, consider the value of your work. Do not delete a file unless you are certain you no longer need the file.

Make sure you only delete files that you have created. Do not delete any files that Windows or other programs require to operate.

DELETE A FILE

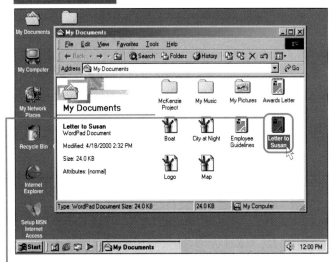

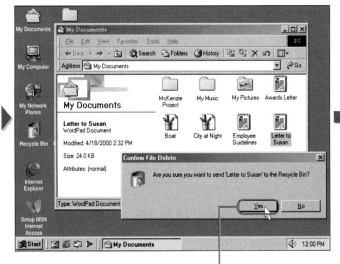

1 Click the file you want to delete.

■ To delete more than one file, select all the files you want to delete.

Note: To select multiple files, see page 58.

2 Press the Delete key.

■ The Confirm File Delete dialog box appears.

3 Click **Yes** to delete the file.

How can I permanently delete a file from my computer?

When you delete a file, Windows places the file in the Recycle Bin in case you later want to restore the file. If you do not want to place a deleted file in the Recycle Bin, you can permanently delete the file from your computer. This is useful when you want to delete a confidential file.

To permanently delete a file, perform steps 1 to 3 on page 72, except press and hold down the Shift key as you perform step 2.

■ The file disappears.

■ Windows places the file in the Recycle Bin in case you later want to restore the file.

Note: To restore a file from the Recycle Bin, see page 74.

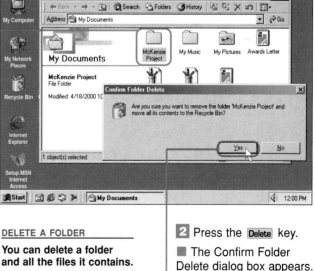

DELETE A FOLDER

You can delete a folder and all the files it contains.

1 Click the folder you want to delete.

2 Press the Delete key.

■ The Confirm Folder Delete dialog box appears.

3 Click **Yes** to delete the folder.

RESTORE A DELETED FILE

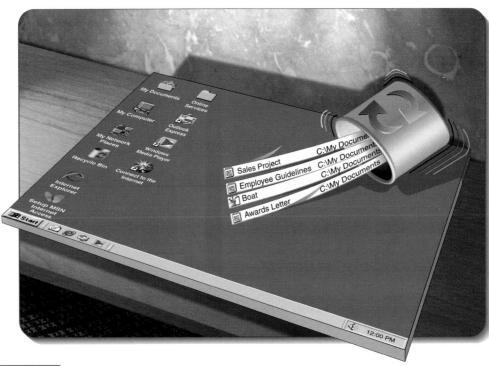

The Recycle Bin stores all the files you have deleted. You can easily restore any of these files to their original location on your computer.

RESTORE A DELETED FILE

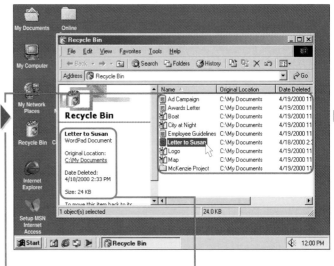

■1 Double-click **Recycle Bin**.

■ The Recycle Bin window appears, displaying all the files you have deleted.

■2 Click the file you want to restore.

■ To restore more than one file, select all the files you want to restore.

Note: To select multiple files, see page 58.

■ This area displays information about the file you selected.

How can I tell if the Recycle Bin contains deleted files?

The appearance of the Recycle Bin indicates whether or not the bin contains deleted files.

Contains deleted files | **Does not contain deleted files**

Why is the file I want to restore not in the Recycle Bin?

You cannot restore files deleted from a floppy disk, removable disk or from locations on your network. Files deleted from these locations are permanently deleted and cannot be restored.

3 Click **File**.

4 Click **Restore**.

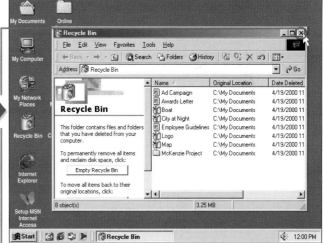

■ The file disappears from the Recycle Bin window. Windows returns the file to its original location on your computer.

5 Click ☒ to close the Recycle Bin window.

Note: You can restore folders the same way you restore files. When you restore a folder, Windows restores all the files in the folder.

EMPTY THE RECYCLE BIN

You can create
more free space
on your computer
by permanently
removing all the
files from the
Recycle Bin.

The Recycle Bin stores all
the files you have deleted.
When you empty the
Recycle Bin, the files are
permanently removed from
your computer and cannot
be restored.

EMPTY THE RECYCLE BIN

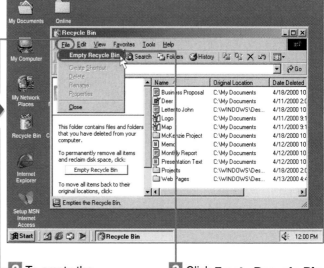

1 Double-click **Recycle Bin**.

■ The Recycle Bin
window appears,
displaying all the files
you have deleted.

2 To empty the
Recycle Bin, click **File**.

3 Click **Empty Recycle Bin**.

**Can I remove only some of the
files from the Recycle Bin?**

You may want to
permanently remove
only a few files from
the Recycle Bin, such
as files that contain
confidential information.

■1 Press and hold down
the **Ctrl** key as you click
each file you want to
permanently remove
from your computer.

■2 Press the **Delete** key.

■ A dialog box will appear
to confirm the deletion.
Click **Yes** to permanently
delete the files.

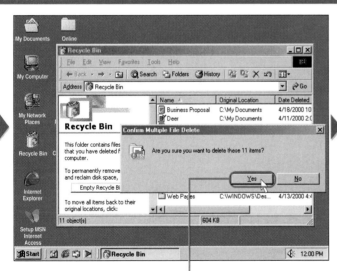

■ The Confirm Multiple
File Delete dialog box
appears.

■4 Click **Yes** to permanently
delete all the files from the
Recycle Bin.

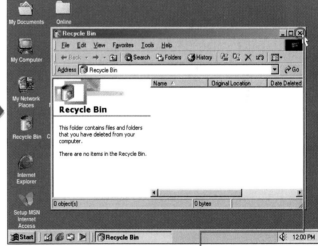

■ Windows permanently
deletes all the files from
your computer.

■5 Click **X** to close
the Recycle Bin window.

CREATE A NEW FILE

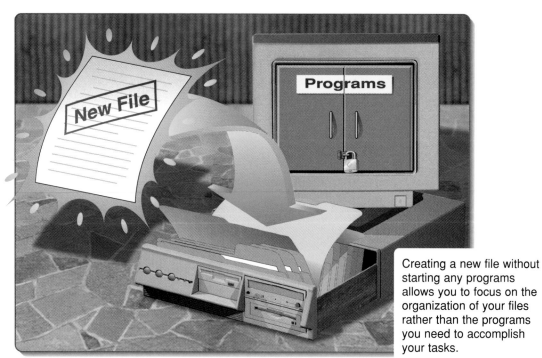

You can instantly create, name and store a new file in the location you want without starting any programs.

Creating a new file without starting any programs allows you to focus on the organization of your files rather than the programs you need to accomplish your tasks.

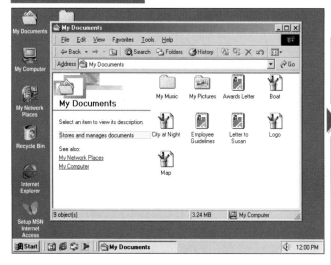

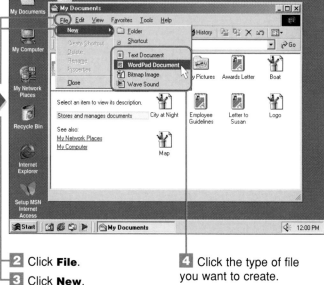

1 Display the contents of the folder you want to contain a new file.

Note: To display the contents of your computer, see page 48.

2 Click **File**.

3 Click **New**.

4 Click the type of file you want to create.

What types of files can I create?

The types of files you can create depend on the programs installed on your computer. By default, Windows allows you to create the following types of files.

📄	Text Document	Allows you to create a document that contains no formatting.
📄	WordPad Document	Allows you to create a document that contains simple formatting.
📄	Bitmap Image	Allows you to create a drawing.
📄	Wave Sound	Allows you to create a sound file.

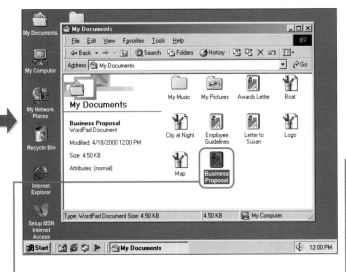

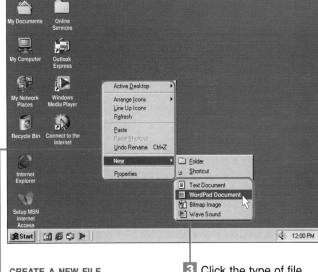

■ The new file appears with a temporary name.

5 Type a name for the new file and then press the **Enter** key.

*Note: A file name cannot contain the \ / : * ? " < > or | characters.*

CREATE A NEW FILE ON THE DESKTOP

1 Right-click a blank area on your desktop. A menu appears.

2 Click **New**.

3 Click the type of file you want to create.

4 Type a name for the new file and then press the **Enter** key.

CREATE A NEW FOLDER

You can create a new folder to help you organize the files stored on your computer. Creating a folder is like placing a new folder in a filing cabinet.

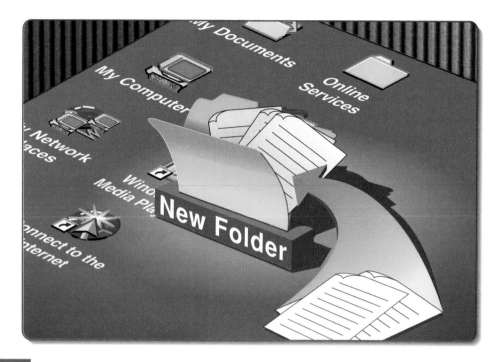

CREATE A NEW FOLDER

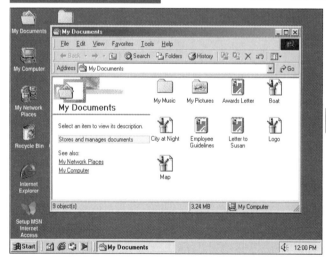

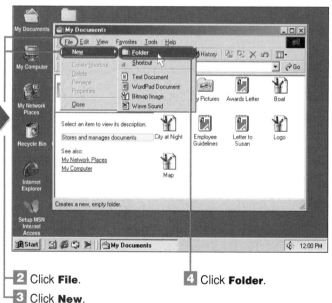

1 Display the contents of the folder you want to contain a new folder.

Note: To display the contents of your computer, see page 48.

2 Click **File**.

3 Click **New**.

4 Click **Folder**.

**How can creating a new folder
help me organize the files on my
computer?**

You can create a new folder to store
files you want to keep together, such
as files for a particular project. This
allows you to quickly locate the files.
For example, you can create a folder
named "Reports" that stores all of
your reports. You can create as many
folders as you need to set up a filing
system that makes sense to you.

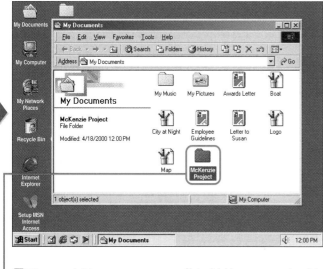

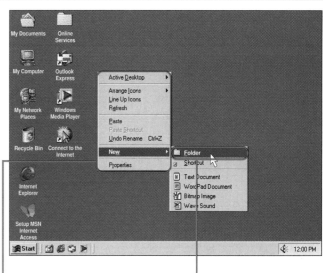

■ The new folder appears,
displaying a temporary name.

5 Type a name for the new
folder and then press the
`Enter` key.

*Note: A folder name cannot contain
the \ / : * ? " < > or | characters.*

**CREATE A NEW FOLDER
ON THE DESKTOP**

1 Right-click an empty
area on your desktop.
A menu appears.

2 Click **New**.

3 Click **Folder**.

4 Type a name for the
new folder and then press
the `Enter` key.

SEARCH FOR FILES

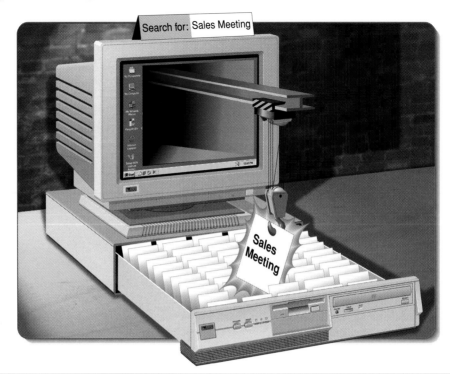

Search for: Sales Meeting

If you cannot remember the exact name or location of a file you want to work with, you can have Windows search for the file on your computer.

SEARCH FOR FILES

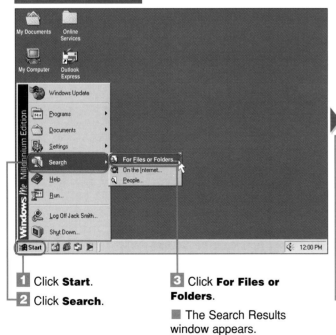

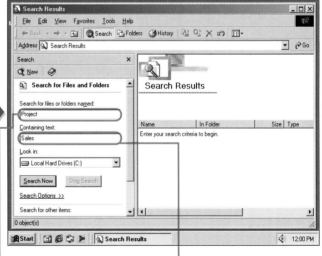

1 Click **Start**.

2 Click **Search**.

3 Click **For Files or Folders**.

■ The Search Results window appears.

SEARCH BY NAME

4 To specify the name of the file you want to find, click this area. Then type all or part of the file name.

SEARCH BY CONTENTS

5 To specify a word or phrase within the file you want to find, click this area. Then type the word or phrase.

How can I search for a file?

Windows offers various ways that you can search for a file, such as by name or by content. You can use all, some or just one of the search methods shown on pages 82 to 85 to find files. Using more search methods will slow down the search but will result in more exact matches.

Can I search for a file if I know only part of the file name?

If you search for part of a file name, Windows will find all the files and folders with names that contain the word you specified. For example, searching for "Report" will find every file or folder with a name containing "Report."

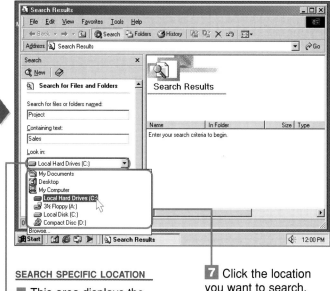

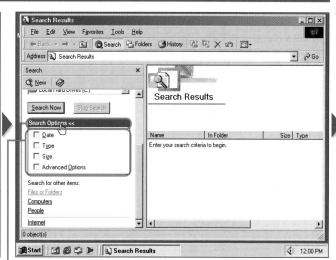

SEARCH SPECIFIC LOCATION

■ This area displays the location Windows will search.

6 Click ▼ in this area to select a different location.

7 Click the location you want to search.

Note: Windows will search all folders within the location you select.

USE ADVANCED SEARCH OPTIONS

8 To use advanced search options, click **Search Options**.

■ Additional search options appear. You may need to use the scroll bar to view all the options.

*Note: To once again hide the additional search options, click **Search Options**.*

CONTINUED ▶

SEARCH FOR FILES

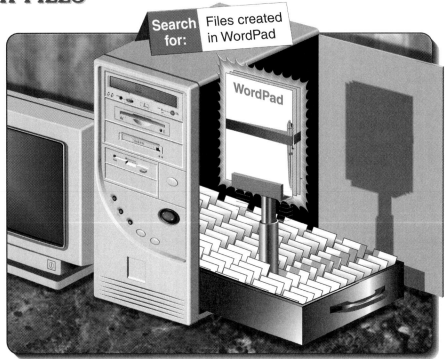

Search for: Files created in WordPad

WordPad

You can search for a file you worked with during a specific time period. You can also search for a specific type of file, such as files you created in WordPad.

SEARCH FOR FILES (CONTINUED)

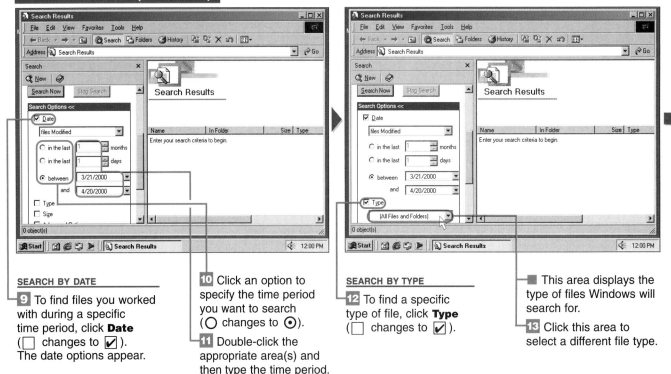

SEARCH BY DATE

9 To find files you worked with during a specific time period, click **Date** (☐ changes to ☑). The date options appear.

10 Click an option to specify the time period you want to search (○ changes to ◉).

11 Double-click the appropriate area(s) and then type the time period.

SEARCH BY TYPE

12 To find a specific type of file, click **Type** (☐ changes to ☑).

■ This area displays the type of files Windows will search for.

13 Click this area to select a different file type.

What types of files can I search for?

You can search for a specific type of file on
your computer to help you narrow your search.
The available file types depend on the programs
installed on your computer. Here is a list of
common file types that you can search for.

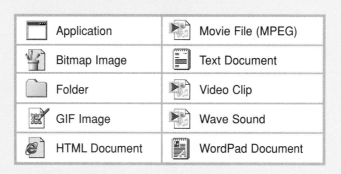

	Application		Movie File (MPEG)
	Bitmap Image		Text Document
	Folder		Video Clip
	GIF Image		Wave Sound
	HTML Document		WordPad Document

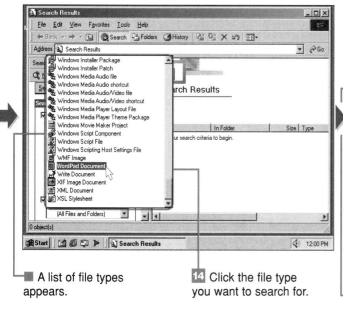

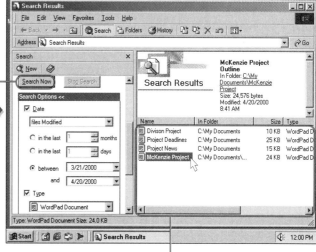

■ A list of file types
appears.

14 Click the file type
you want to search for.

START THE SEARCH

15 To start the search,
click **Search Now**.

■ This area displays the
names of the matching
files Windows found and
information about each file.

16 To open a file,
double-click the name
of the file.

ADD A SHORTCUT TO THE DESKTOP

You can add a
shortcut to the
desktop that will
provide a quick
way of opening
a file you use
regularly.

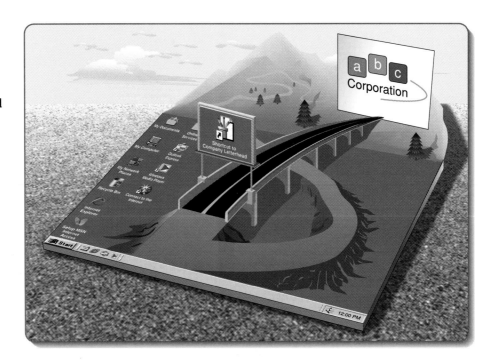

ADD A SHORTCUT TO THE DESKTOP

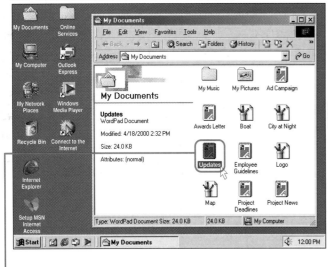

1 Click the file you want
to create a shortcut to.

2 Click **File**.

3 Click **Send To**.

4 Click **Desktop
(create shortcut)**.

How do I rename or delete a shortcut?

You can rename or delete a shortcut the same way you would rename or delete any file. Renaming or deleting a shortcut will not affect the original file. To rename a file, see page 66. To delete a file, see page 72.

Rename   Delete

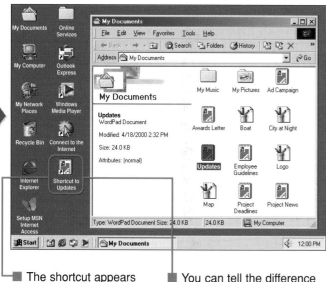

■ The shortcut appears on your desktop.

■ You can tell the difference between the shortcut and the original file because the shortcut icon displays an arrow ( ).

■ You can double-click the shortcut to open the file.

Note: You can create a shortcut to a folder the same way you create a shortcut to a file. Creating a shortcut to a folder will give you quick access to all the files in the folder.

CHAPTER 6

Customize Windows

This chapter will show you how to personalize your computer by adding a desktop theme, wallpaper or adjusting your mouse settings.

MOVE THE TASKBAR

You can move the taskbar to a different location on your screen.

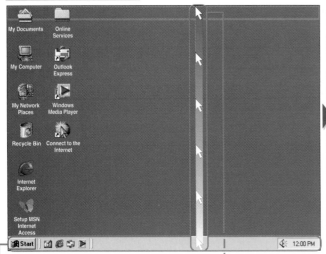

■ By default, Windows displays the taskbar at the bottom of your screen.

1 To move the taskbar, position the mouse ⏳ over a blank area on the taskbar.

2 Drag the taskbar to a new location on your screen.

■ The taskbar moves to the new location.

Note: You can move the taskbar to the top, bottom, left or right edge of your screen.

90

RESIZE THE TASKBAR

You can change
the size of the
taskbar to display
more information
on the taskbar.

RESIZE THE TASKBAR

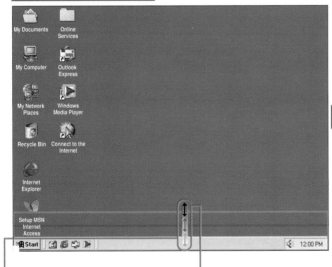

1 Position the mouse ⌖
over the edge of the
taskbar (⌖ changes to ↕).

2 Drag the mouse ↕
until the taskbar displays
the size you want.

■ The taskbar changes
to the new size.

HIDE THE TASKBAR

You can temporarily hide the taskbar to provide more room on your screen to accomplish tasks.

HIDE THE TASKBAR

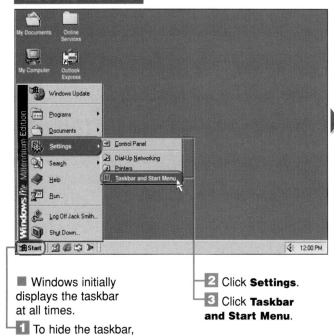

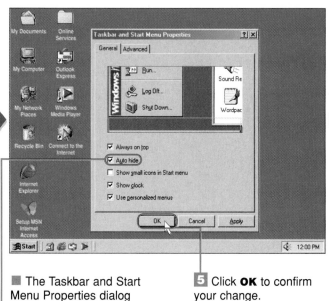

■ Windows initially displays the taskbar at all times.

1 To hide the taskbar, click **Start**.

2 Click **Settings**.

3 Click **Taskbar and Start Menu**.

■ The Taskbar and Start Menu Properties dialog box appears.

4 Click **Auto hide** to hide the taskbar when you are not using the taskbar (☐ changes to ☑).

5 Click **OK** to confirm your change.

What information does the taskbar display?

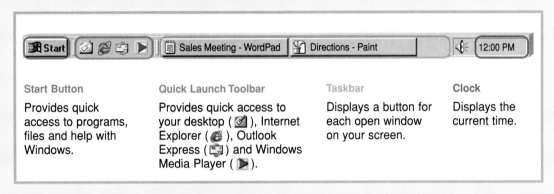

Start Button

Provides quick access to programs, files and help with Windows.

Quick Launch Toolbar

Provides quick access to your desktop ( ), Internet Explorer ( ), Outlook Express ( ) and Windows Media Player ( ).

Taskbar

Displays a button for each open window on your screen.

Clock

Displays the current time.

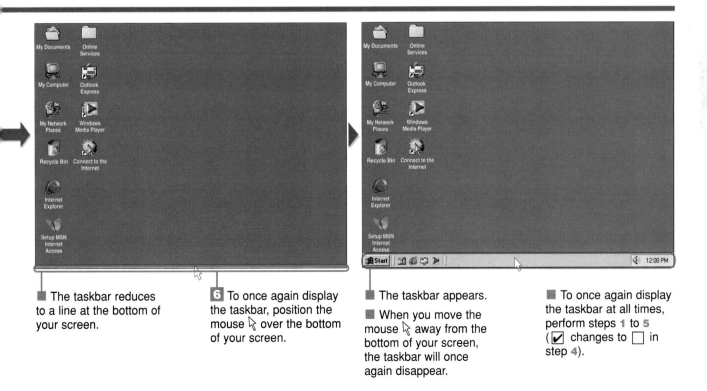

■ The taskbar reduces to a line at the bottom of your screen.

6 To once again display the taskbar, position the mouse over the bottom of your screen.

■ The taskbar appears.

■ When you move the mouse away from the bottom of your screen, the taskbar will once again disappear.

■ To once again display the taskbar at all times, perform steps **1** to **5** (changes to in step **4**).

93

ADD WALLPAPER

You can decorate
your screen by
adding wallpaper.

ADD WALLPAPER

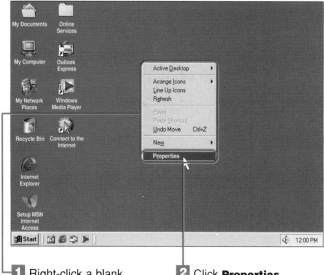

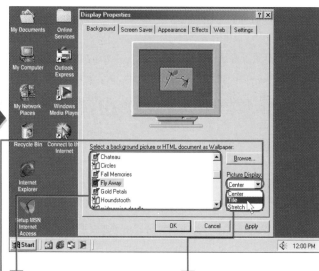

1 Right-click a blank
area on your desktop.
A menu appears.

2 Click **Properties**.

■ The Display Properties
dialog box appears.

3 Click the wallpaper
you want to use to
decorate your screen.

4 Click this area to
select how you want to
display the wallpaper
on your screen.

5 Click the way you want
to display the wallpaper.

*Note: For more information,
see the top of page 95.*

How can I display wallpaper on my screen?

Center

Places the wallpaper in the middle of your screen.

Tile

Repeats the wallpaper until it fills your entire screen.

Stretch

Stretches the wallpaper to cover the entire screen.

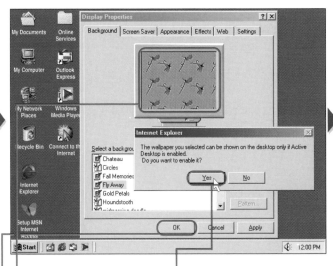

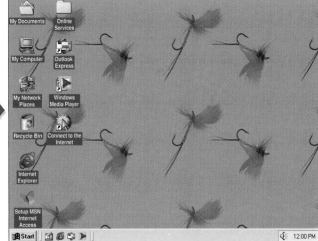

■ This area displays how the wallpaper will appear on your screen.

6 Click **OK** to add the wallpaper to your screen.

■ A dialog box appears if the wallpaper you selected requires you to enable the Active Desktop feature.

7 Click **Yes** to enable the Active Desktop feature.

■ The wallpaper appears on your screen.

■ To remove wallpaper from your screen, perform steps **1** to **3**, selecting **(None)** in step **3**. Then perform step **6**.

SET UP A SCREEN SAVER

A screen saver is a moving picture or pattern that appears on the screen when you do not use your computer for a period of time.

SET UP A SCREEN SAVER

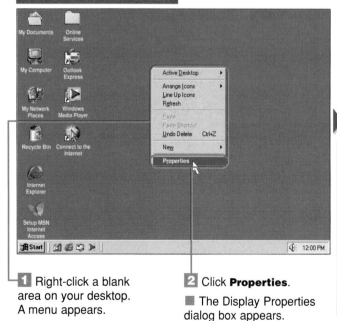

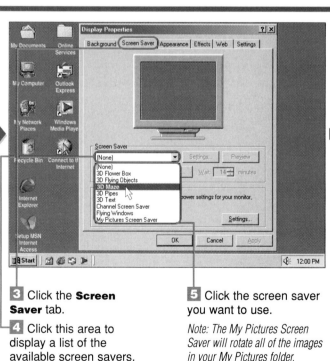

1 Right-click a blank area on your desktop. A menu appears.

2 Click **Properties**.

■ The Display Properties dialog box appears.

3 Click the **Screen Saver** tab.

4 Click this area to display a list of the available screen savers.

5 Click the screen saver you want to use.

Note: The My Pictures Screen Saver will rotate all of the images in your My Pictures folder.

Do I need to use a screen saver?

Screen savers were originally designed to prevent screen burn, which occurs when an image appears in a fixed position on the screen for a period of time. Today's monitors are less susceptible to screen burn, but people still use screen savers for their entertainment value.

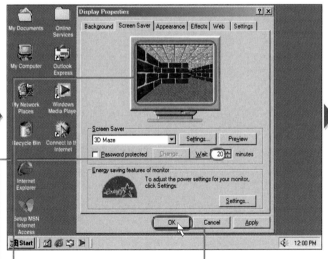

■ This area displays a preview of how the screen saver will appear on your screen.

6 To specify the number of minutes your computer must be inactive before the screen saver will appear, double-click this area. Then type the number of minutes.

7 Click **OK** to confirm your changes.

■ The screen saver appears when you do not use your computer for the number of minutes you specified.

■ You can move the mouse or press a key on the keyboard to remove the screen saver from your screen.

■ To turn off the screen saver, perform steps **1** to **5**, selecting **(None)** in step **5**. Then perform step **7**.

CHANGE SCREEN COLORS

You can change the colors displayed on your screen to personalize and enhance Windows.

CHANGE SCREEN COLORS

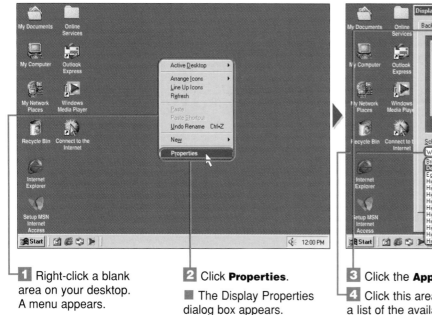

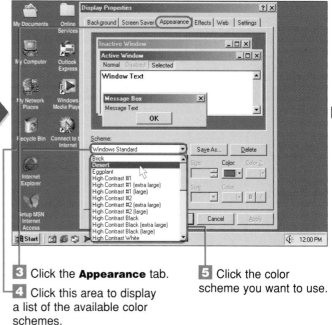

1 Right-click a blank area on your desktop. A menu appears.

2 Click **Properties**.

■ The Display Properties dialog box appears.

3 Click the **Appearance** tab.

4 Click this area to display a list of the available color schemes.

5 Click the color scheme you want to use.

What is the difference between the high contrast, high color and VGA color schemes?

High Contrast

High contrast color schemes are designed for people with vision impairments.

High Color

High color schemes are designed for computers displaying more than 256 colors.

VGA

VGA color schemes are designed for computers limited to 16 colors.

For information on changing the number of colors your computer can display, see page 102.

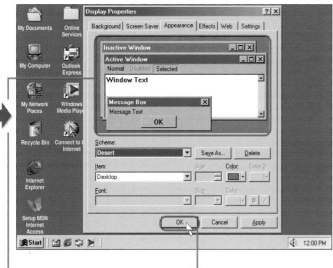

■ This area displays how your screen will look with the color scheme you selected.

6 Click **OK** to change the color scheme.

■ The desktop displays the color scheme you selected.

■ To return to the original color scheme, perform steps **1** to **6**, selecting **Windows Standard** in step **5**.

CHANGE THE DATE AND TIME

You should make sure the correct date and time are set in your computer. Windows uses the date and time to determine when you create and update your files.

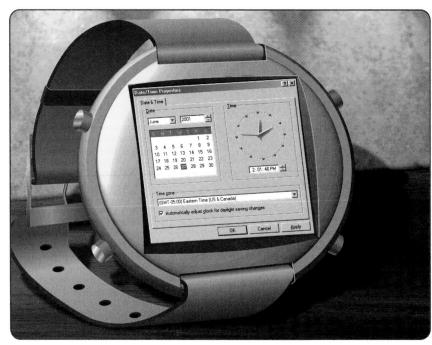

CHANGE THE DATE AND TIME

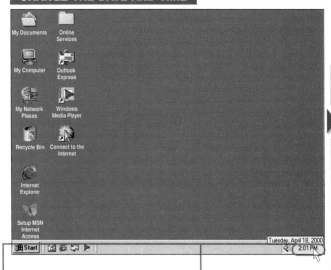

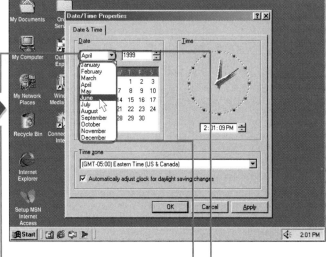

■ This area displays the time set in your computer.

1 To display the date set in your computer, position the mouse ⅃ over this area. After a moment, the date appears.

2 To change the date or time set in your computer, double-click this area.

■ The Date/Time Properties dialog box appears.

■ This area displays the month set in your computer.

3 To change the month, click this area.

4 Click the correct month.

100

Will Windows keep track of the date and time even when I turn off my computer?

Yes. Your computer has a built-in clock that keeps track of the date and time even when you turn off your computer.

Will Windows ever change the time automatically?

Windows will change the time automatically to compensate for daylight saving time. When you turn on your computer after daylight saving time occurs, Windows will display a message indicating that the time was changed.

New clock settings
Windows has updated your clock as a result of Daylight Saving Time. Please verify that your new clock settings are correct.

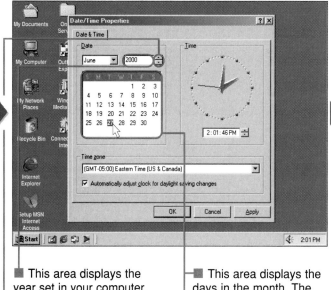

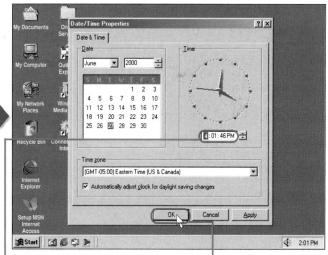

■ This area displays the year set in your computer.

5 To change the year, click ▲ or ▼ in this area until the correct year appears.

■ This area displays the days in the month. The current day is highlighted.

6 To change the day, click the correct day.

■ This area displays the time set in your computer.

7 To change the time, double-click the part of the time you want to change. Then type the correct information.

8 Click **OK** to confirm your changes.

CHANGE COLOR DEPTH

You can change the number of colors displayed on your screen. More colors result in higher quality images.

Your monitor and video card determine the maximum number of colors your screen can display.

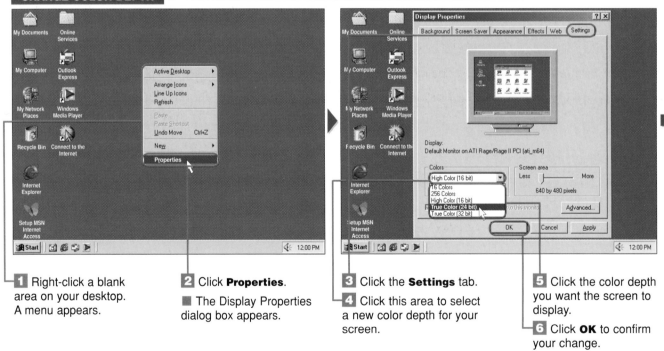

1 Right-click a blank area on your desktop. A menu appears.

2 Click **Properties**.

■ The Display Properties dialog box appears.

3 Click the **Settings** tab.

4 Click this area to select a new color depth for your screen.

5 Click the color depth you want the screen to display.

6 Click **OK** to confirm your change.

When would I change the number of colors displayed on my screen?

You may want to display more colors on your screen when viewing photographs, playing videos or playing games on your computer. Windows offers the following color depths.

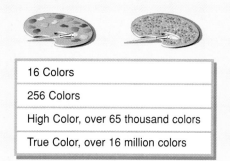

16 Colors
256 Colors
High Color, over 65 thousand colors
True Color, over 16 million colors

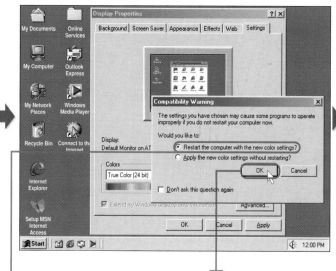

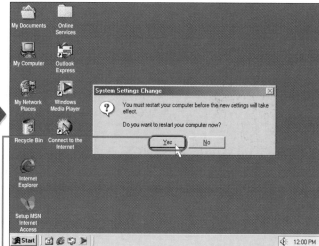

■ A dialog box appears, stating that some programs may not operate properly if you do not restart your computer.

7 Click this option to restart your computer with the new color settings (○ changes to ⊙).

8 Click **OK** to restart your computer.

■ A dialog box appears, stating that you must restart your computer before the new color settings will take effect.

9 Click **Yes** to restart your computer.

■ When your computer restarts, Windows will use the new color settings you specified.

CHANGE SCREEN RESOLUTION

You can change the
screen resolution to
adjust the amount
of information that
can fit on your
screen.

Your monitor
and video card
determine which
screen resolutions
you can use.

CHANGE SCREEN RESOLUTION

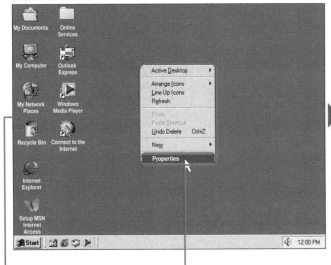

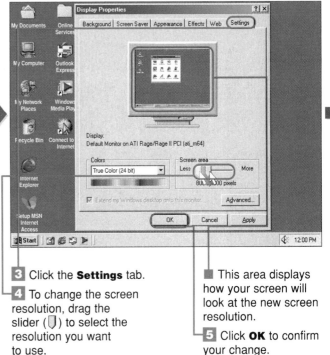

1 Right-click a blank
area on your desktop.
A menu appears.

2 Click **Properties**.

■ The Display Properties
dialog box appears.

3 Click the **Settings** tab.

4 To change the screen
resolution, drag the
slider ( ) to select the
resolution you want
to use.

■ This area displays
how your screen will
look at the new screen
resolution.

5 Click **OK** to confirm
your change.

Which screen resolution should I use?

The screen resolution is measured by the number of horizontal and vertical pixels displayed on a screen. A pixel is the smallest point on a screen. The most common screen resolutions are 640 by 480 pixels and 800 by 600 pixels.

Lower screen resolutions display larger images so you can see the information on your screen more clearly.

Higher screen resolutions display smaller images so you can display more information on your screen at once.

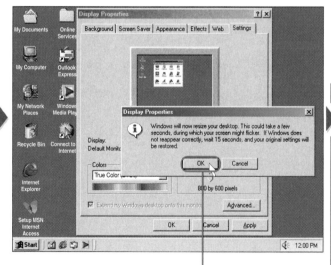

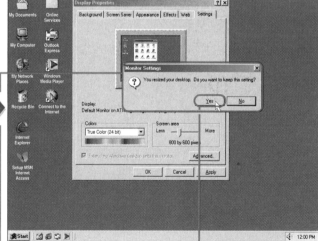

■ A dialog box appears, stating that Windows will take a few seconds to change the screen resolution. Your screen may flicker during this time.

6 Click **OK** to change the screen resolution.

■ Windows resizes the information on your screen.

■ The Monitor Settings dialog box appears, asking if you want to keep the new screen resolution.

7 Click **Yes** to keep the screen resolution.

CHANGE MOUSE SETTINGS

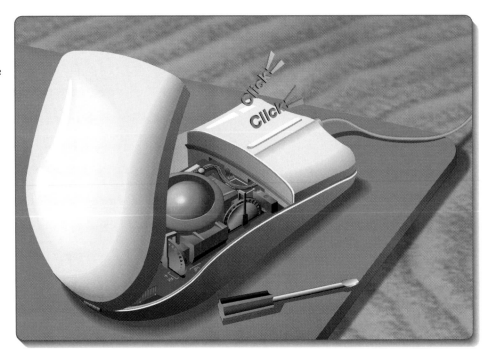

You can change the way your mouse works to suit your individual needs.

CHANGE MOUSE SETTINGS

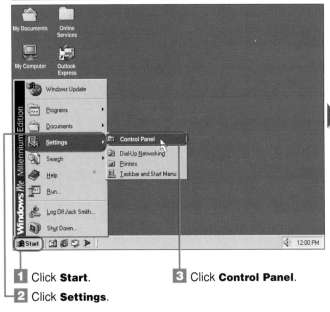

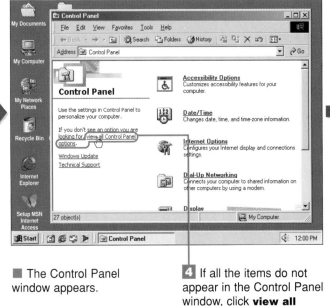

1 Click **Start**.

2 Click **Settings**.

3 Click **Control Panel**.

■ The Control Panel window appears.

4 If all the items do not appear in the Control Panel window, click **view all Control Panel options** to display all the items.

Should I use a mouse pad?

A mouse pad provides a smooth surface for moving the mouse on your desk. You should use a mouse pad to reduce the amount of dirt that enters the mouse and protect your desk from scratches. Hard plastic mouse pads attract less dirt and provide a smoother surface than fabric mouse pads.

My mouse pointer does not move smoothly on my screen. What can I do?

You may need to clean your mouse. Turn the mouse over and remove and clean the roller ball. Then use a cotton swab to remove the dirt from the rollers inside the mouse.

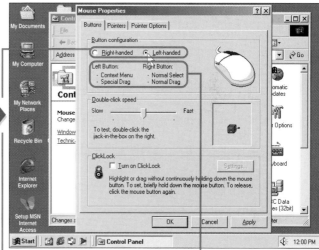

■ All of the items appear in the Control Panel window.

5 Double-click **Mouse** to change the mouse settings.

■ The Mouse Properties dialog box appears.

SWITCH MOUSE BUTTONS

6 To switch the functions of the left and right mouse buttons, click an option to specify if you are right-handed or left-handed (○ changes to ⊙).

■ This area describes the functions of the left and right mouse buttons, depending on the option you selected.

CONTINUED

107

CHANGE MOUSE SETTINGS

You can personalize the way your mouse works by changing the double-click speed. You can also change the appearance of the mouse pointers Windows displays.

Double-click Speed

Pointer Appearance

CHANGE MOUSE SETTINGS (CONTINUED)

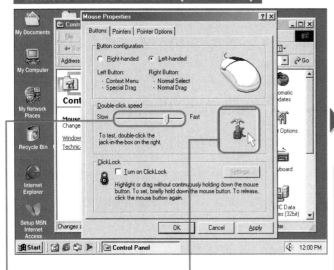

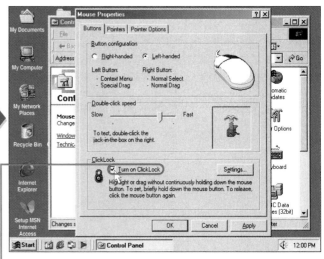

DOUBLE-CLICK SPEED

7 To change the amount of time that can pass between two clicks of the mouse button for Windows to recognize a double-click, drag the slider (⬚) to a new position.

8 Double-click this area to test the double-click speed.

■ The jack-in-the-box appears if you clicked at the correct speed.

CLICKLOCK

9 To select or drag information without having to continuously hold down the mouse button, click this option (☐ changes to ✔).

108

How can I use the ClickLock mouse setting to select text?

The ClickLock mouse setting allows you to select text without having to continuously hold down the mouse button as you select the text. To select text using ClickLock, perform the following steps.

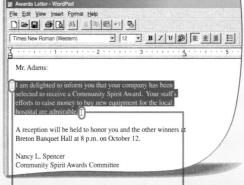

1 Position the mouse I to the left of the text you want to select.

2 Briefly press and hold down the mouse button. Then release the mouse button.

3 Position the mouse I at the end of the text you want to select and then click the mouse button again.

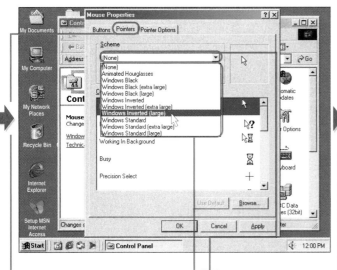

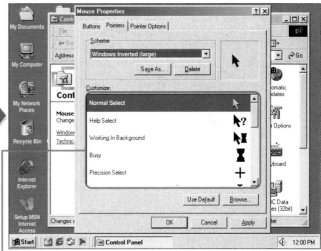

POINTER APPEARANCE

10 To change the appearance of the mouse pointers, click the **Pointers** tab.

11 Click this area to display a list of the mouse pointer sets.

12 Click the mouse pointer set you want to use.

■ This area displays the mouse pointers that make up the set you selected.

Note: The mouse pointer assumes different shapes, depending on its location on your screen and the task you are performing.

CONTINUED

CHANGE MOUSE SETTINGS

You can change how
fast the mouse pointer
moves on your screen.
You can also have
the mouse pointer
automatically appear
over the default button
in many dialog boxes.

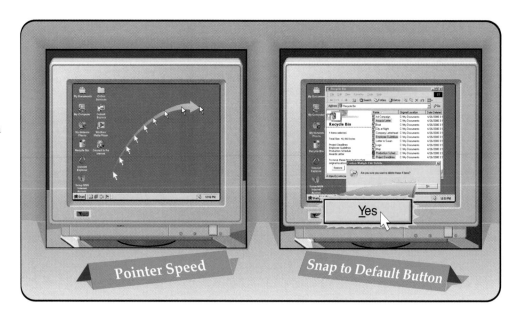

Pointer Speed

Snap to Default Button

CHANGE MOUSE SETTINGS (CONTINUED)

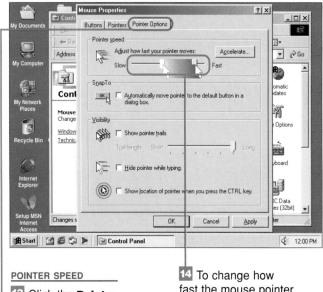

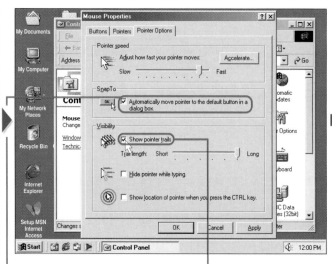

POINTER SPEED

13 Click the **Pointer
Options** tab.

14 To change how
fast the mouse pointer
moves on your screen,
drag the slider (⬇) to
a new position.

SNAP TO DEFAULT BUTTON

15 To have the mouse
pointer automatically appear
over the default button in
many dialog boxes, click this
option (☐ changes to ☑).

*Note: The default button in many
dialog boxes is **OK**.*

SHOW POINTER TRAILS

16 To leave a trail
of mouse pointers as
you move the mouse
around your screen,
click this option
(☐ changes to ☑).

How can I make the mouse pointer easier to see on my screen?

Windows offers two options that can help you more clearly see the mouse pointer on your screen. These options are especially useful on portable computer screens where the mouse pointer can be difficult to follow.

Show pointer trails

Displays mouse pointer trails to help you follow the movement of the mouse pointer on your screen.

Show pointer location

Shows the location of the mouse pointer when you press the `Ctrl` key. Moving circles will appear around the mouse pointer to help you quickly locate the pointer on your screen.

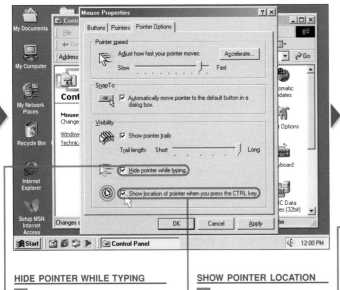

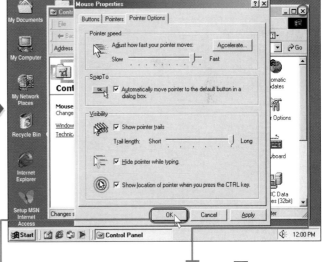

HIDE POINTER WHILE TYPING

17 To hide the mouse pointer when you type, click this option (☐ changes to ✔).

Note: The mouse pointer will reappear when you move the mouse.

SHOW POINTER LOCATION

18 To show the location of the mouse pointer when you press the `Ctrl` key, click this option (☐ changes to ✔).

CONFIRM CHANGES

19 When you finish changing the mouse settings, click **OK**.

20 Click ☒ to close the Control Panel window.

USING DESKTOP THEMES

You can use a desktop theme to customize the appearance of your desktop. Windows offers several themes, including a baseball, jungle and mystery theme.

USING DESKTOP THEMES

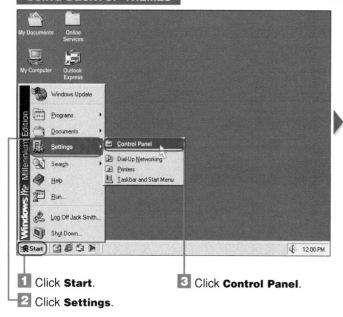

1 Click **Start**.

2 Click **Settings**.

3 Click **Control Panel**.

■ The Control Panel window appears.

4 If all the items do not appear in the Control Panel window, click **view all Control Panel options** to display all the items.

Why doesn't the Desktop Themes item appear in the Control Panel window?

When you first install Windows, the Desktop Themes feature is not automatically added to your computer. To add the Desktop Themes feature, you must add the Desktop Themes component to your computer. To add a Windows component, see page 170.

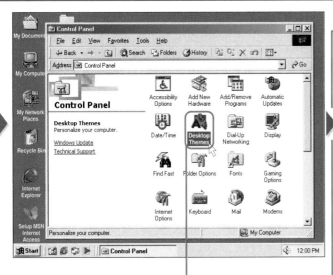

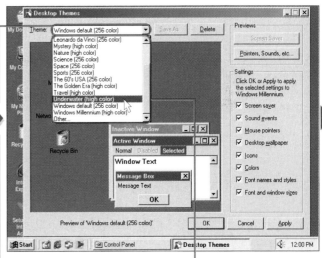

■ All of the items appear in the Control Panel window.

5 Double-click **Desktop Themes**.

Note: If the Desktop Themes item is not displayed, see the top of this page.

■ The Desktop Themes window appears.

6 Click this area to display a list of the available desktop themes.

7 Click the desktop theme you want to use.

CONTINUED

USING DESKTOP THEMES

Windows provides a screen saver for each desktop theme.

A screen saver is a moving picture or pattern that appears on the screen when you do not use your computer for a period of time.

USING DESKTOP THEMES (CONTINUED)

■ This area displays a preview of the theme you selected.

8 To display a preview of the screen saver for the theme, click **Screen Saver**.

■ A preview of the screen saver appears on your screen.

9 To remove the screen saver from your screen, move the mouse or press a key on your keyboard.

When I use a desktop theme, which settings will change on my computer?

A desktop theme will change many settings on your computer. Here are some examples.

Sound events

Windows will play sound effects when you perform certain tasks on your computer.

Mouse pointers

Windows will use a collection of mouse pointers that change depending on the task you are performing.

Desktop wallpaper

Windows will display a colorful design on your desktop.

Icons

Windows will use decorative pictures for the items on your desktop.

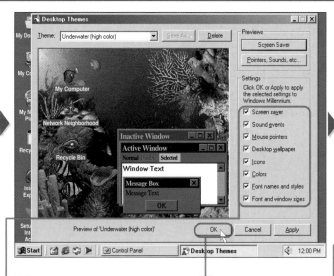

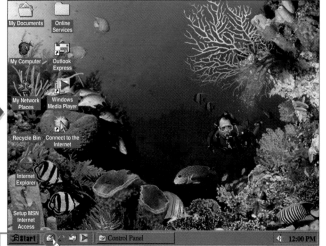

10 Windows will apply the theme you selected to each setting that displays a check mark (✔). You can click a setting to add (✔) or remove (☐) a check mark.

11 Click **OK** to confirm your changes.

■ Windows applies the desktop theme you selected.

12 Click 🔲 to minimize all open windows so you can clearly view your desktop.

■ To return to the original desktop theme, perform steps **1** to **7** starting on page 112, selecting **Windows default** in step **7**. Then press the Enter key.

ADD AN ACTIVE DESKTOP ITEM

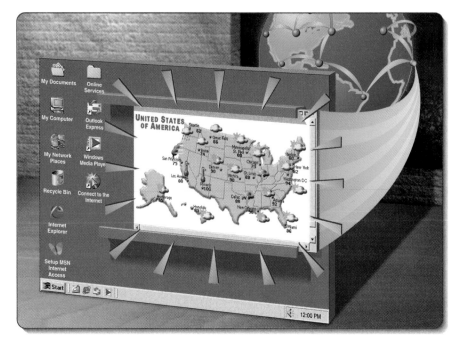

You can add active content from the Web to your desktop. Active content is information that constantly changes on your screen, such as a stock ticker or a weather map.

ADD AN ACTIVE DESKTOP ITEM

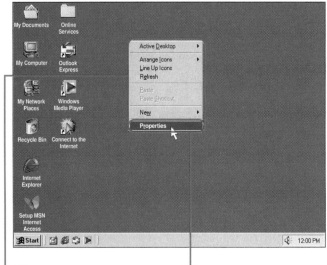

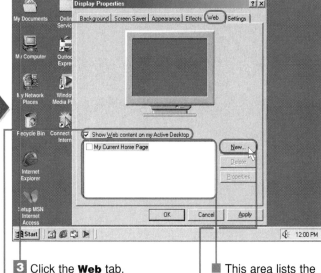

1 Right-click a blank area on your desktop. A menu appears.

2 Click **Properties**.

■ The Display Properties dialog box appears.

3 Click the **Web** tab.

4 Click this option to be able to add Active Desktop items to your desktop (☐ changes to ☑).

■ This area lists the Active Desktop items currently available on your computer.

5 Click **New** to add a new Active Desktop item to your desktop.

What is the "My Current Home Page" item that appears in the list of Active Desktop items?

The My Current Home Page item will display your home page on your desktop. Your home page is the Web page that appears each time you start the Internet Explorer Web browser.

Why does a Security Warning dialog box appear when I display the Desktop Gallery Web page?

If the Security Warning dialog box appears when you display the Desktop Gallery Web page, Microsoft needs to transfer information to your computer. Click **Yes** to transfer the information to your computer.

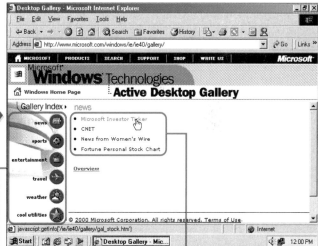

■ The New Active Desktop Item dialog box appears.

6 To visit the Desktop Gallery on the Internet where you can find Active Desktop items, click **Visit Gallery**.

*Note: If you are not connected to the Internet, a dialog box appears that allows you to connect. Click **Connect** to connect to the Internet.*

■ The Microsoft Internet Explorer window opens and displays the Desktop Gallery Web page.

Note: To maximize the window to fill your screen, click ▣ in the top right corner of the window.

7 Click a category to display Active Desktop items of interest.

■ This area displays the Active Desktop items in the category you selected.

8 Click an Active Desktop item of interest.

CONTINUED

ADD AN ACTIVE DESKTOP ITEM

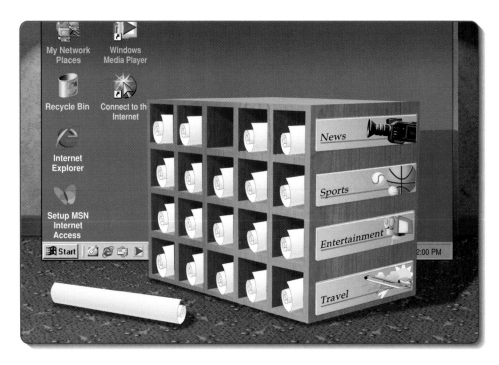

The Desktop Gallery Web page offers various types of Active Desktop items that you can add to your desktop.

ADD AN ACTIVE DESKTOP ITEM (CONTINUED)

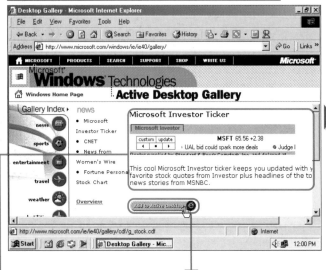

■ Information about the Active Desktop item you selected appears.

Note: You can repeat steps 7 and 8 on page 117 to view information about other Active Desktop items.

9 To add the displayed Active Desktop item to your desktop, click **Add to Active Desktop**.

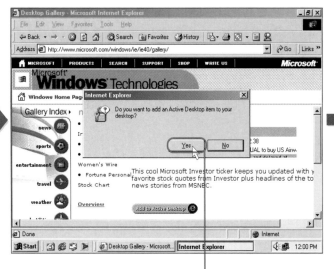

■ A dialog box appears, asking if you want to add the Active Desktop item to your desktop.

10 Click **Yes** to add the Active Desktop item to your desktop.

How can I change the size of an Active Desktop item on my desktop?

You can change the size of an Active Desktop item on your desktop by performing the following steps.

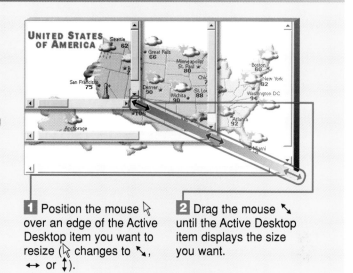

1 Position the mouse ⬛ over an edge of the Active Desktop item you want to resize (⬛ changes to ⬛, ↔ or ↕).

2 Drag the mouse ⬛ until the Active Desktop item displays the size you want.

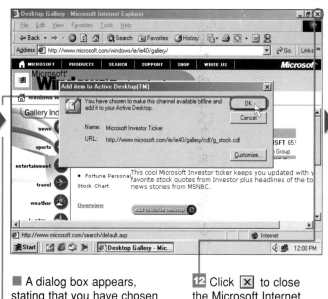

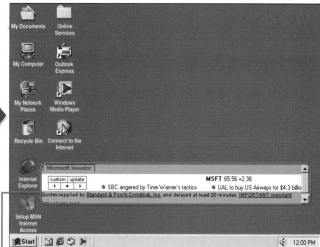

■ A dialog box appears, stating that you have chosen to add the Active Desktop item to your desktop.

11 Click **OK** to continue.

■ Windows copies the necessary information to your computer.

12 Click ✕ to close the Microsoft Internet Explorer window.

*Note: A dialog box may appear, asking if you want to disconnect from the Internet. Click **Disconnect Now** to disconnect.*

■ The Active Desktop item appears on your desktop.

■ The Active Desktop item will update automatically only when you are connected to the Internet.

Note: To move or hide the Active Desktop item, see pages 120 and 121.

MOVE AN ACTIVE DESKTOP ITEM

You can move an Active Desktop item to a different location on your screen.

MOVE AN ACTIVE DESKTOP ITEM

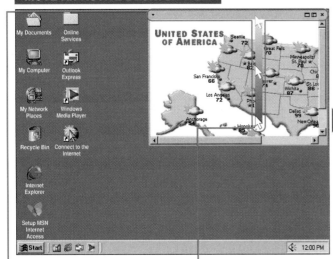

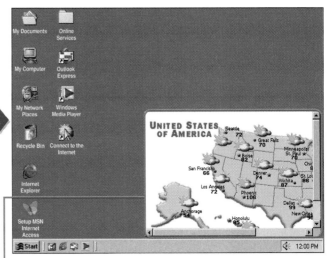

1 Position the mouse ⬚ over the top edge of the Active Desktop item you want to move. A gray bar appears.

2 Position the mouse ⬚ over the gray bar.

3 Drag the mouse ⬚ to where you want to place the Active Desktop item.

■ The Active Desktop item appears in the new location.

120

HIDE OR DISPLAY AN ACTIVE DESKTOP ITEM

You can temporarily hide an Active Desktop item you no longer want to appear on your screen. You can redisplay the item at any time.

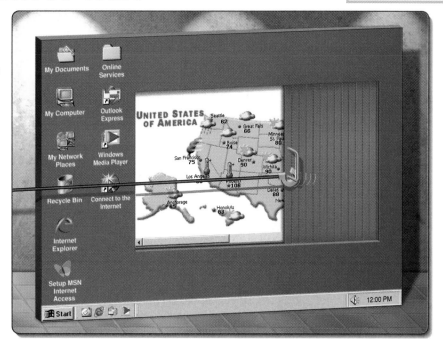

HIDE OR DISPLAY AN ACTIVE DESKTOP ITEM

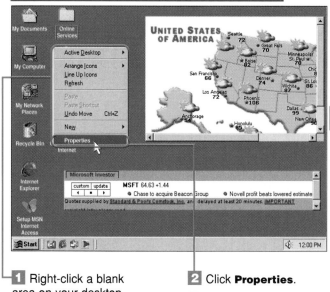

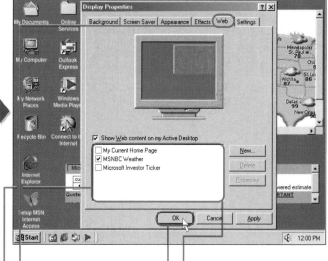

1 Right-click a blank area on your desktop. A menu appears.

2 Click **Properties**.

■ The Display Properties dialog box appears.

3 Click the **Web** tab.

■ This area lists the Active Desktop items available on your computer.

4 Each item that displays a check mark (☑) appears on your desktop. Click the box beside an item you want to hide (☐) or display (☑).

5 Click **OK** to confirm your change.

CHAPTER 7

Have Fun with Windows

In this chapter you will find out how to play music CDs, listen to Internet radio stations and play games.

PLAY GAMES

Windows includes several games that you can play on your computer. Games are a fun way to improve your mouse skills and hand-eye coordination.

You can also play games, such as Checkers, with other people on the Internet. Windows will match you with other players from around the world. To play, you will need an Internet connection.

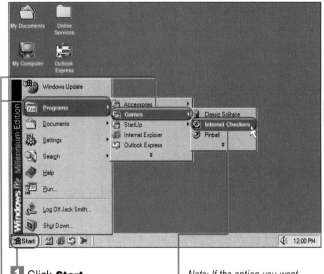

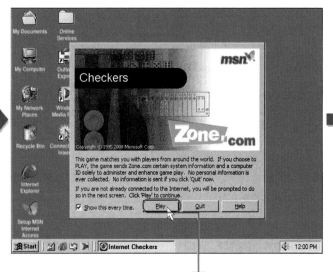

1 Click **Start**.

2 Click **Programs**.

3 Click **Games**.

Note: If the option you want is not displayed on a menu, position the mouse ⬚ over the bottom of the menu to display all the options.

4 Click the game you want to play.

■ If you selected an Internet game, a dialog box appears, displaying information about playing games on the Internet.

Note: If you selected a non-Internet game, skip to step 7.

5 Click **Play** to continue.

124

What games are included with Windows?

Here are some popular games included with Windows.

Classic Solitaire

Solitaire is a classic card game that you play on your own. The object of the game is to place all the cards in order from ace to king in four stacks, one stack for each suit.

Minesweeper

Minesweeper is a strategy game in which you try to avoid being blown up by mines.

Pinball

Pinball is similar to a pinball game you would find at an arcade. You launch a ball and then try to score as many points as possible.

■ If you are not currently connected to the Internet, the Connect To dialog box appears.

■ This area displays your user name and password.

Note: A symbol (ˣ) appears for each character in your password to prevent others from viewing the password.

6 Click **Connect** to connect to the Internet.

■ A window appears, displaying the game. In this example, the Internet Checkers window appears.

7 When you finish playing the game, click ☒ to close the window.

■ If you are playing an Internet game, a message will appear to confirm that you want to leave the game. Click **Yes** to leave the game.

ASSIGN SOUNDS TO PROGRAM EVENTS

Windows can play sound effects when you perform certain tasks on your computer.

You need a sound card and speakers to play sound effects on your computer.

ASSIGN SOUNDS TO PROGRAM EVENTS

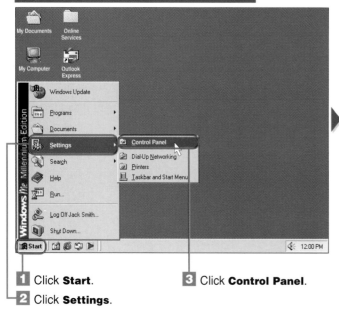

1 Click **Start**.

2 Click **Settings**.

3 Click **Control Panel**.

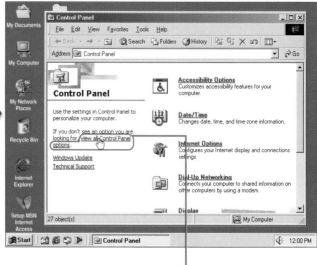

■ The Control Panel window appears.

4 If all the items do not appear in the Control Panel window, click **view all Control Panel options** to display all the items.

What events can Windows assign sounds to?

Windows can assign sounds to over 30 events
on your computer. Here are some examples.

Exit Windows

A sound will play each
time you exit Windows.

tjones@abc.com

New Mail Notification

A sound will play each time you
receive a new e-mail message.

Empty Recycle Bin

A sound will play each time
you empty the Recycle Bin.

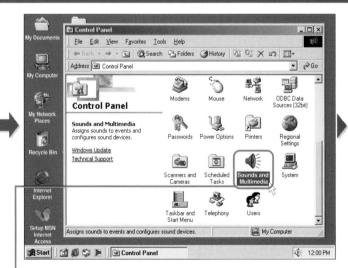

■ All of the items appear
in the Control Panel
window.

*Note: You may need to scroll
through the window to display
the Sounds and Multimedia item.*

5 Double-click **Sounds
and Multimedia**.

■ The Sounds and
Multimedia Properties
dialog box appears.

■ This area lists the
events to which you
can assign sounds.

CONTINUED

ASSIGN SOUNDS TO PROGRAM EVENTS

When assigning
sounds to program
events, you can test
the sound that will
play for each event.

ASSIGN SOUNDS TO PROGRAM EVENTS (CONTINUED)

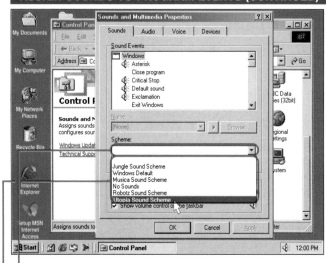

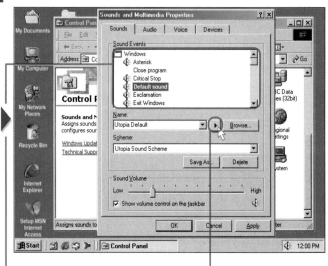

6 Click this area to display
a list of sound schemes.
Each sound scheme will
change the sounds for
many events at once.

7 Click the sound scheme
you want to use.

*Note: To add more sound schemes
to your computer, see the top of
page 129.*

■ A dialog box may appear,
asking if you want to save
the previous sound scheme.
To continue without saving,
click **No**.

■ A speaker icon (🔊)
appears beside each
event that will play a
sound.

8 To play the sound for
an event, click the event.

9 Click ▶ to play
the sound.

Does Windows provide additional sound schemes?

When you first install Windows, all the sound schemes that Windows provides are not automatically added to your computer. You can later add additional sound schemes by adding the Multimedia Sound Schemes component to your computer. To add Windows components, see page 170. You will find the Multimedia Sound Schemes component in the Multimedia category.

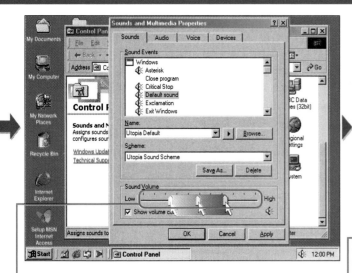

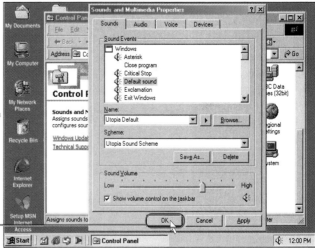

10 To change the volume of the sound, drag this slider ( ) left or right to decrease or increase the volume.

Note: Changing the volume in this dialog box will adjust the volume for all sounds on your computer, such as sound from a music CD or video.

11 Click **OK** to confirm your changes.

■ To stop Windows from playing sounds for events, perform steps **1** to **7**, selecting **No Sounds** in step **7**. Then perform step **11**.

PLAY A MUSIC CD

You can use
your computer
to play music
CDs while you
work.

You need a
CD-ROM drive,
a sound card
and speakers to
play music CDs.

PLAY A MUSIC CD

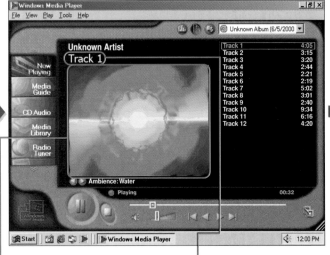

1 Insert a music CD
into your CD-ROM drive.

■ The Windows Media
Player window appears
and the CD begins to
play.

2 Click 🔲 to maximize
the Windows Media
Player window to fill your
screen.

■ This area displays a
graphical representation of
the song that is currently
playing.

■ This area displays the
number of the song that
is currently playing.

**How can I play a music CD
while performing other tasks
on my computer?**

If you want to perform other
tasks on your computer while
playing a music CD, minimize
the Windows Media Player
window to remove the window
from your screen. To minimize
a window, see page 15.

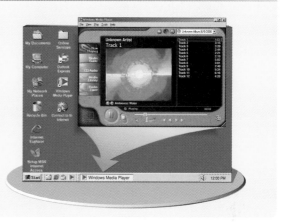

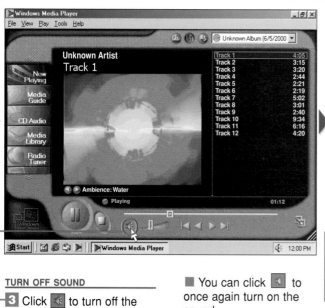

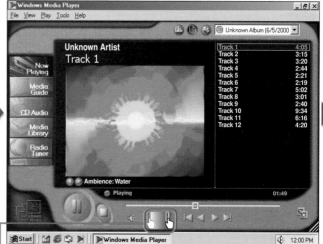

TURN OFF SOUND

3 Click ◄ to turn off the
sound (◄ changes to ◄).

■ You can click ◄ to
once again turn on the
sound.

CHANGE SOUND VOLUME

4 To change the
volume of the sound,
drag the slider (▯) left
or right to decrease or
increase the volume.

*Note: The volume also depends
on the volume set by using the
speaker icon (◄) on the taskbar.
To use the speaker icon to change
the volume, see page 134.*

CONTINUED

PLAY A MUSIC CD

When playing a music CD, you can play a different song or view the list of songs on the CD.

PLAY A MUSIC CD (CONTINUED)

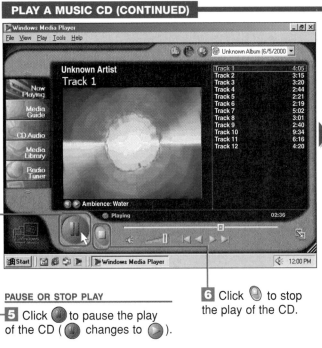

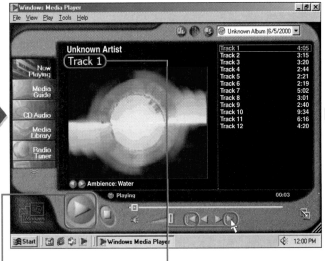

PAUSE OR STOP PLAY

5 Click 🔘 to pause the play of the CD (🔘 changes to ▶️).

6 Click 🔘 to stop the play of the CD.

RESUME PLAY

7 Click ▶️ to resume the play of the CD.

PLAY ANOTHER SONG

■ This area displays which song is currently playing.

8 Click one of the following options to play another song on the CD.

◀️ Play the previous song

▶️ Play the next song

Can I listen to a music CD privately?

You can listen to a music CD privately by plugging headphones into the jack at the front of your CD-ROM drive. If your CD-ROM drive does not have a headphone jack, you can plug the headphones into the back of your computer where you normally plug in the speakers.

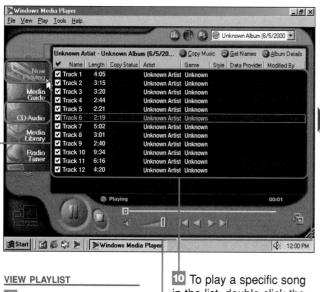

VIEW PLAYLIST

■9 Click the **CD Audio** tab to view a list of the songs on the CD.

■ This area displays a list of the songs on the CD.

■10 To play a specific song in the list, double-click the song.

■11 To once again display the graphical representation of the current song, click the **Now Playing** tab.

CLOSE WINDOWS MEDIA PLAYER

■12 When you finish listening to the music CD, click ⊠ to close the Windows Media Player window.

■13 Remove the music CD from your CD-ROM drive.

ADJUST THE VOLUME

You can easily adjust the volume of sound coming from your speakers.

Adjusting the volume will affect all the sounds you play on your computer, such as sound from a music CD or a video.

ADJUST THE VOLUME

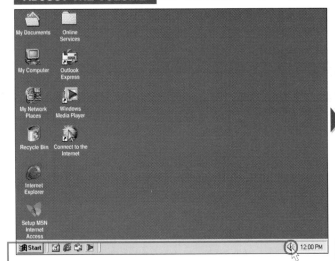

1 Click 🔊 to display the volume control box.

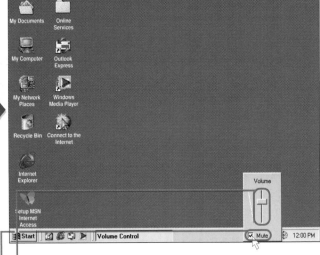

2 Drag the slider (▭) up or down to increase or decrease the volume.

3 Click this option to turn off the sound (☐ changes to ☑). The speaker icon 🔊 changes to 🔇 on the taskbar.

Note: You can repeat step 3 to once again turn on the sound.

4 To hide the volume control box, click outside the box.

DISPLAY MEDIA PLAYER IN COMPACT MODE

When using Windows Media Player to play sound or video files, you can switch to the compact mode, which takes up less room on your screen.

The compact mode offers fewer features than the full mode, but provides more room on your screen for using other programs.

DISPLAY MEDIA PLAYER IN COMPACT MODE

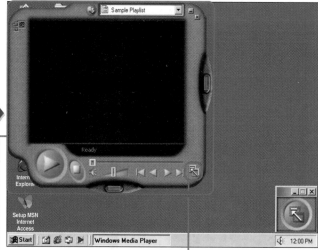

1 Click ▶ to start Windows Media Player.

■ The Windows Media Player window appears.

2 Click 🔲 to switch to the compact mode of Windows Media Player.

■ Windows Media Player appears in the compact mode.

■ To once again display Windows Media Player in the full mode, click 🔲.

LISTEN TO RADIO STATIONS ON THE INTERNET

You can use Windows Media Player to listen to radio stations from around the world that broadcast on the Internet.

You need a sound card, speakers and an Internet connection to listen to radio stations that broadcast on the Internet.

LISTEN TO RADIO STATIONS ON THE INTERNET

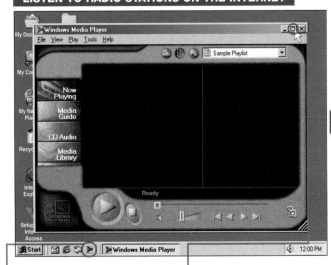

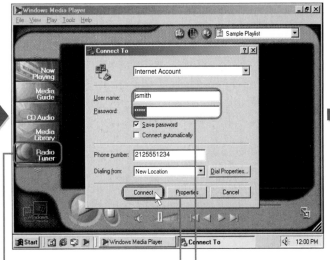

1 Click ▶ to start Windows Media Player.

■ The Windows Media Player window appears.

2 Click □ to maximize the window to fill your screen.

3 Click the **Radio Tuner** tab to listen to radio stations on the Internet.

■ If you are not currently connected to the Internet, the Connect To dialog box appears.

■ This area displays your user name and password.

Note: A symbol (x) appears for each character in your password to prevent others from viewing the password.

4 Click **Connect** to connect to the Internet.

How does Windows play radio stations that broadcast on the Internet?

Before a radio station that broadcasts on the Internet begins to play, the information is partially transferred and temporarily stored in a section of memory on your computer called a buffer. While the radio station plays, information will continuously transfer from the Internet and be temporarily stored in the buffer. This ensures that any interruptions to the information transferring on the Internet will not cause interruptions to the radio station playing on your computer.

■ This area displays a list of radio stations that you can listen to.

5 Double-click the name of the radio station you want to listen to.

■ After a moment, the radio station begins to play.

■ The Web page for the radio station appears as a button on the taskbar. To display the Web page, click its button on the taskbar.

Note: To remove the Web page from your screen, click ☒ *in the top right corner of the window.*

6 To change the volume, drag the slider (▯) left or right to decrease or increase the volume.

7 To stop playing the radio station, click ●.

CONTINUED

LISTEN TO RADIO STATIONS ON THE INTERNET

You can search for radio stations that broadcast on the Internet.

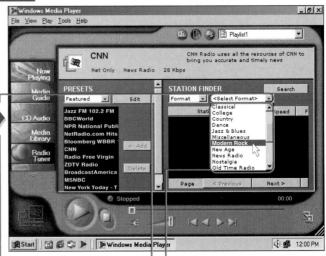

SEARCH FOR RADIO STATIONS

■ Click this area to list the ways you can search for radio stations.

2 Click the way you want to search for radio stations.

Note: For information on the ways you can search for radio stations, see the top of page 139.

■ An area appears that allows you to specify which radio stations you want to search for.

3 Click this area to list the options for the search method you chose in step **2**.

4 Click the option you want to use.

■ A list of options will not appear if you selected Callsign, Frequency or Keyword in step **2**. To specify the information you want to search for, click this area and type the information. Then press the Enter key.

138

How can I search for radio stations that broadcast on the Internet?

Search By	Description
Format	Type of music such as Oldies, Religious or Rock.
Band	Band such as AM, FM or Internet Only.
Language	Language such as English, French or Russian.
Location	Location such as Canada, United States or Japan.
Callsign	Call letters for a station, such as CNN.
Frequency	Frequency for a station, such as 102.3.
Keyword	Words in the slogan of a station, such as "rock and roll" or "timely news."

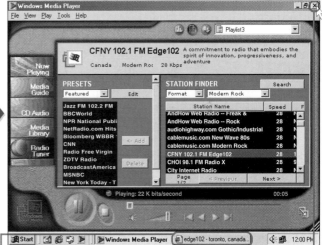

■ This area displays the radio stations that match the information you specified.

5 Double-click the radio station of interest.

■ After a moment, the radio station begins to play.

■ The Web page for the radio station appears as a button on the taskbar. To display the Web page, click its button on the taskbar.

Note: To remove the Web page from your screen, click ✕ *in the top right corner of the window.*

6 When you finish listening to radio stations, click ✕ to close the Windows Media Player window.

*Note: A dialog box will appear, asking if you want to disconnect from the Internet. Click **Disconnect Now** to disconnect.*

USING THE MEDIA GUIDE

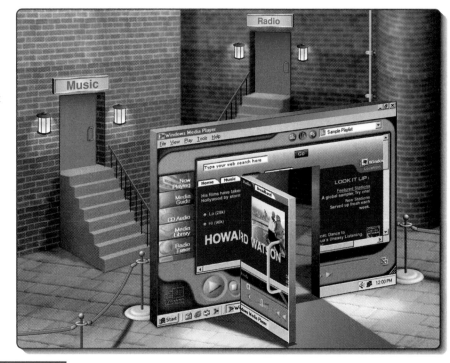

You can use the Media Guide to access the latest music, movies and videos on the Internet.

You must have a connection to the Internet to use the Media Guide.

USING THE MEDIA GUIDE

1 Click ▶ to start Windows Media Player.

■ The Windows Media Player window appears.

2 Click □ to maximize the window to fill your screen.

3 Click the **Media Guide** tab.

■ If you are not currently connected to the Internet, the Connect To dialog box appears.

■ This area displays your user name and password.

Note: A symbol (×) appears for each character in your password to prevent others from viewing the password.

4 Click **Connect** to connect to the Internet.

When using the Media Guide, how can I reduce the time it takes for information to appear on my screen?

You can get a faster connection to the Internet to reduce the time it takes for information to transfer to your computer and appear on your screen. Most people use a modem to connect to the Internet, although you can get a faster connection by using a cable modem, Integrated Services Digital Network (ISDN) line or Digital Subscriber Line (DSL). Unlike a modem, these connection methods do not use your telephone line, which allows you to use your computer while leaving your telephone line available for telephone calls.

■ This area displays the Media Guide. The Media Guide is a Web page that is updated daily to provide access to the latest music, movies and videos on the Internet.

Note: The Media Guide on your screen may look different than the screen shown above.

5 Click a tab to display information for a particular type of media.

6 Click a topic of interest to display more information on the topic.

■ Information on the topic you selected appears.

7 You can repeat step **6** until you find information of interest.

8 When you finish using the Media Guide, click ⌧ to close the Windows Media Player window.

*Note: A dialog box will appear, asking if you want to disconnect from the Internet. Click **Disconnect Now** to disconnect.*

ORGANIZE YOUR MEDIA FILES

You can use the Media Library to organize all the media files on your computer.

A media file can be a sound or video file.

ORGANIZE YOUR MEDIA FILES

1 Click ▶ to start Windows Media Player.

■ The Windows Media Player window appears.

2 Click ☐ to maximize the window to fill your screen.

3 Click the **Media Library** tab.

■ The first time you visit the Media Library, a dialog box appears, asking if you want to search your computer for media files.

4 Click **Yes** to search your computer for media files.

Note: If the dialog box does not appear and you want to search your computer for media files, press the **F3** *key and then skip to step **5**.*

Where can I obtain media files?

Media Guide

You can use the Media Guide that Windows provides to access the latest music, movies and videos on the Internet. For information on the Media Guide, see page 140.

The Internet

Many Web sites on the Internet offer sound and video files. You can find sound and video files at the following Web sites:

www.jurassicpunk.com
earthstation1.com
soundamerica.com
wavcentral.com

Computer Stores

Many computer stores offer collections of sound and video files that you can purchase.

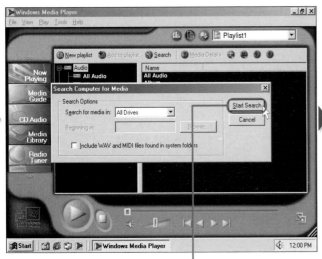

■ The Search Computer for Media dialog box appears.

5 Click **Start Search** to start the search.

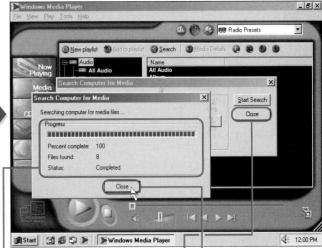

■ Windows searches your computer for media files.

■ This area shows the progress of the search.

6 When the search is complete, click **Close** to close the dialog box.

7 Click **Close** to close the Search Computer for Media dialog box.

CONTINUED

ORGANIZE YOUR MEDIA FILES

You can play sound and video files that are listed in the Media Library.

ORGANIZE YOUR MEDIA FILES (CONTINUED)

■ The Media Library organizes your collection of media files into categories.

■ A category displaying a plus sign (⊞) contains hidden items.

1 To display the items in a category, click the plus sign (⊞) beside the category (⊞ changes to ⊟).

■ The item(s) in the category appear.

Note: To once again hide the items in a category, click the minus sign (⊟) beside the category.

2 Click the category that contains the media files of interest.

■ This area displays the media files in the category you selected.

3 To play a media file, double-click the file.

How does the Media Library organize my sound and video files?

The Media Library organizes your sound and video files into several categories.

Audio	
All Audio	Lists all of your sound files.
Album	Organizes sound files by album.
Artist	Organizes sound files by artist.
Genre	Organizes sound files by type, such as Soundtrack.

Video	
All Clips	Lists all of your video files.
Author	Organizes video files by author.

■ If you selected a video file, the video appears in this area.

4 To change the volume, drag the slider (⬛) left or right to decrease or increase the volume.

Note: The volume also depends on the volume set by using the speaker icon (◁⌇) on the taskbar. To use the speaker icon to change the volume, see page 134.

■ This area shows the progress of the sound or video file.

5 To stop playing the sound or video file, click ◯.

■ You can click the **Media Library** tab to return to your list of media files.

6 When you finish working with your media files, click ☒ to close the Windows Media Player window.

CHANGE SKIN OF MEDIA PLAYER

You can change the skin of Windows Media Player to customize how the player looks and functions.

CHANGE SKIN OF MEDIA PLAYER

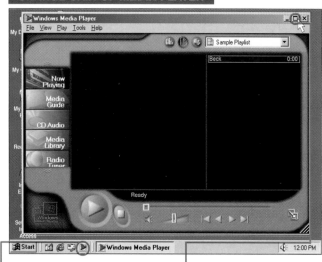

1 Click ▶ to start Windows Media Player.

■ The Windows Media Player window appears.

2 Click ⬜ to maximize the window to fill your screen.

3 To change the skin of Windows Media Player, click the **Skin Chooser** tab.

■ If the Skin Chooser tab is not displayed, click this arrow until the tab appears.

■ This area lists the available skins that you can use with Windows Media Player.

4 Click the skin you want to use.

Where can I obtain more skins for Windows Media Player?

You can obtain more skins for Windows Media Player on the Internet.

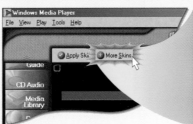 

When working with skins in Windows Media Player, click **More Skins**. If you are not connected to the Internet, a dialog box will appear, asking you to connect.

Windows will open Microsoft Internet Explorer and display a Web page that offers a list of skins that you can use. When you find and select the skin you want to use, the skin will transfer to your computer and appear in your list of available skins.

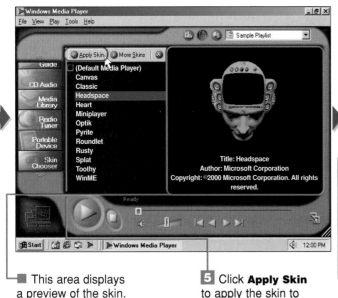

■ This area displays a preview of the skin.

5 Click **Apply Skin** to apply the skin to Windows Media Player.

■ Windows Media Player appears in the compact mode and displays the skin you selected.

Note: Windows Media Player can display the skin only when in the compact mode. For more information on the compact and full modes, see page 135.

■ To once again display Windows Media Player in the full mode, click ▣.

Note: The location of ▣ changes, depending on the skin you selected.

147

Create Movies

In this chapter you will learn how to record, play and edit your own videos with Windows Movie Maker.

You can use Windows Movie Maker to transfer your home movies to your computer. You can then organize and edit the movies before sharing them with friends and family.

Before using Windows Movie Maker, you need to install and set up the equipment needed to transfer your home movies to your computer.

Cables

You will need one or more cables to connect the video camera or other video source to your computer. Video capture cards often come with the cables you need. If you do not have the cables you need, you can purchase the appropriate cables at most computer stores.

Video Source

You can transfer movies from a video camera onto your computer. You can also transfer movies from a Web camera, television broadcast, VCR or DVD player onto your computer.

Video Capture Card

A video capture card must be installed inside your computer to transfer movies from your video camera onto your computer. A video capture card that also allows you to watch television on your computer is known as a TV tuner card. If you are using a newer digital video camera, you may be able to install a firewire card instead of a video capture card for better performance.

You will also need to install a video capture card if you are transferring movies from a television broadcast, VCR or DVD player. If you are using a Web camera, you may not need to install a video capture card.

Other Computer Requirements

Your computer must have the following minimum requirements for Windows Movie Maker to work properly.

300 MHz Pentium II or equivalent

64 MB of memory

2 GB of free hard disk space

You can start Windows Movie Maker to create and work with movies on your computer.

START WINDOWS MOVIE MAKER

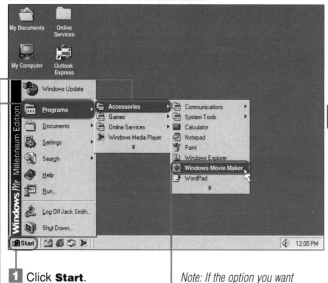

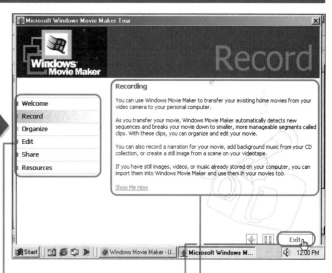

1 Click **Start**.

2 Click **Programs**.

3 Click **Accessories**.

Note: If the option you want is not displayed on a menu, position the mouse ⟆ over the bottom of the menu to display all the options.

4 Click **Windows Movie Maker**.

■ The Microsoft Windows Movie Maker Tour appears the first time you start Windows Movie Maker.

5 Click a topic of interest.

■ This area displays information about the topic you selected.

6 When you finish reviewing information in the Microsoft Windows Movie Maker Tour, click **Exit**.

RECORD A VIDEO

You can record video from your video camera or other video source onto your computer.

Before you start recording, make sure your video source is at the point where you want to begin recording.

RECORD A VIDEO

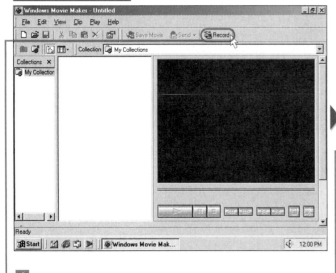

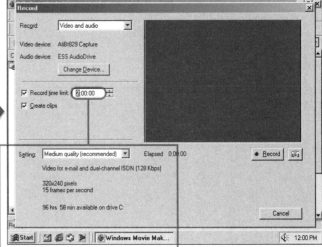

1 Click **Record** to record your video onto your computer.

■ The Record dialog box appears.

■ This area displays the total amount of time that you can record video.

2 To change the amount of time, click the part of the time you want to change and then type a new number.

Note: Windows Movie Maker will automatically stop recording after the time period you specify. The default recording time is set at two hours.

What quality setting should I use to record my video?

When selecting a quality setting for your video, you should consider your intended audience and how people will view your movie. For example, if people will view your movie on the Internet or in an e-mail message, consider the time the movie will take to transfer to a person's computer. The higher the quality setting, the longer a movie will take to transfer. When recording a video, the goal is to create the smallest file size without sacrificing the video quality.

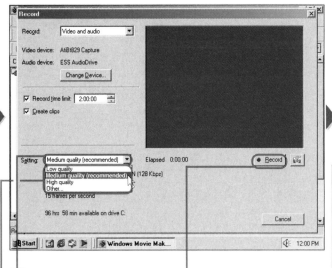

3 Click this area to display a list of the available quality settings that you can use to record the video.

4 Click the quality setting you want to use.

Note: For information on the quality setting that you should use, see the top of this page.

5 Click **Record** to start recording.

■ The word **Recording** blinks in this area when Windows Movie Maker begins recording the video.

6 Press the play button on your video camera or other video source that provides the video you want to record.

CONTINUED

RECORD A VIDEO

Windows automatically stores each video you record in the My Videos folder on your computer. This folder is located within the My Documents folder on your desktop.

Windows creates the My Videos folder the first time you start Windows Movie Maker on your computer.

RECORD A VIDEO (CONTINUED)

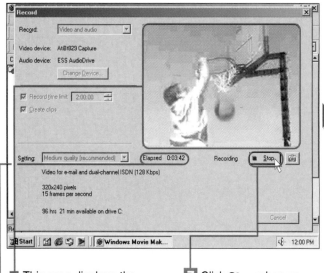

■ This area displays the video.

■ This area displays the time that has passed since you started recording the video.

7 Click **Stop** when you want to stop recording the video.

8 Press the stop button on your video camera or other video source to stop the video.

■ The Save Windows Media File dialog box appears.

9 Type a name for your video.

■ This area shows the location where Windows Movie Maker will store your video. You can click this area to change the location.

10 Click **Save** to save the video.

How does Windows Movie Maker organize videos that I record?

Collections

Each time you record a video, Windows Movie Maker creates a collection to store all the clips for the video.

Clips

Windows Movie Maker automatically breaks up a video you record into smaller, more manageable segments, called clips. A clip is created each time Windows detects an entirely different sequence in a video, such as when you turn on your video camera or when you switch from pause and begin recording.

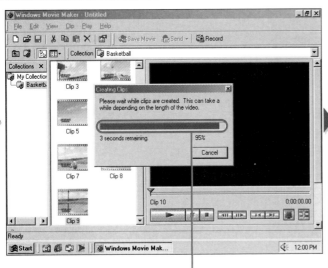

■ The Creating Clips dialog box appears while Windows Movie Maker creates the clips for your video. For information on clips, see the top of this page.

■ This area shows the progress of the creation of the clips.

■ When Windows Movie Maker has finished creating the clips for your video, this area displays a folder that stores the collection of video clips. The name of the collection is the name you specified in step 9.

■ This area displays the video clips within the collection.

PLAY A VIDEO CLIP

You can play each video clip you have recorded on your computer.

Playing video clips helps you determine which clips you want to include in your movie.

PLAY A VIDEO CLIP

1 Click the collection that contains the video clip you want to play.

2 Click the video clip you want to play.

3 Click ▭ to play the video clip.

■ The video clip plays in this area.

4 You can click one of these buttons to pause (⫾⫾) or stop (■) the video clip at any time.

Note: To once again play the video clip, repeat steps 2 and 3.

■ This arrow (▼) indicates the progress of the video clip.

ADD A VIDEO CLIP TO STORYBOARD

You must add each video clip that you want to include in your movie to the storyboard.

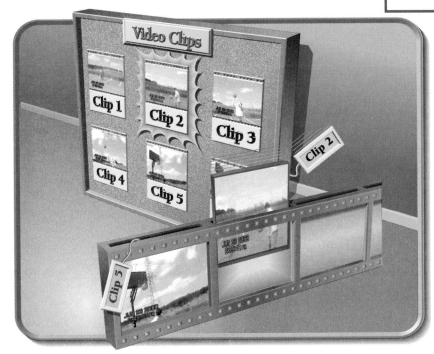

The storyboard displays the order in which video clips will appear in your movie.

ADD A VIDEO CLIP TO STORYBOARD

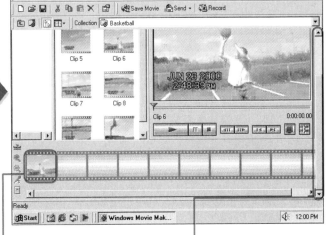

1 Click the collection that contains the video clip you want to add to the storyboard.

2 Click the video clip you want to add.

3 Click **Clip**.

4 Click **Add To Storyboard/Timeline**.

■ The video clip appears on the storyboard.

■ You may need to use the scroll bar to view the storyboard.

■ You can repeat steps **1** to **4** for each video clip you want to add to the storyboard.

REMOVE A VIDEO CLIP FROM STORYBOARD

If you no longer want
to include a video clip
in your movie, you can
remove the video clip
from the storyboard.

REMOVE A VIDEO CLIP FROM STORYBOARD

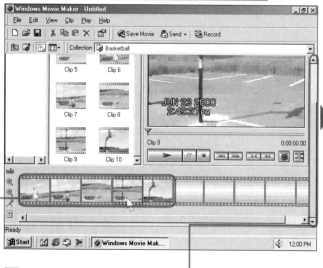

1 Click the video clip on
the storyboard that you want
to remove from your movie.

■ If you do not see the
storyboard, you can use
the scroll bar to view the
storyboard.

2 Press the Delete key.

■ The video clip disappears
from the storyboard.

Note: Deleting a video clip from
the storyboard does not remove
the video clip from Windows
Movie Maker.

REARRANGE VIDEO CLIPS ON STORYBOARD

You can change the order of video clips on the storyboard.

The order of video clips on the storyboard determines the order in which the clips will appear in your movie.

REARRANGE VIDEO CLIPS ON STORYBOARD

1 Position the mouse over the video clip on the storyboard that you want to move to a different location.

■ If you do not see the storyboard, you can use the scroll bar to view the storyboard.

2 Drag the video clip to a new location. A vertical bar indicates the new location.

■ The video clip appears in the new location.

■ The surrounding video clips automatically move to make room for the video clip.

SAVE A PROJECT

You can save a project so you can later review and make changes to the project.

A project is a rough draft of your movie that contains all the video clips you added to the storyboard. You should regularly save changes you make to a project to avoid losing your work.

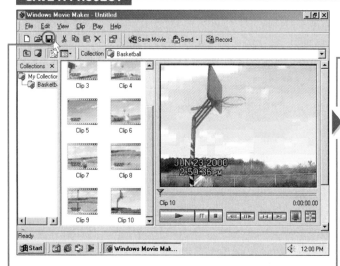

1 Click 🖫 to save your project.

■ The Save Project dialog box appears.

Note: If you previously saved your project, the Save Project dialog box will not appear since you have already named the project.

2 Type a name for your project.

■ This area shows the location where Windows Movie Maker will store your project. You can click this area to change the location.

3 Click **Save** to save your project.

You can open a
saved project to
display its contents
on your screen.
Opening a project
allows you to
review and make
changes to the
project.

A project is a
rough draft of
your movie that
contains all the
video clips you
added to the
storyboard.

OPEN A PROJECT

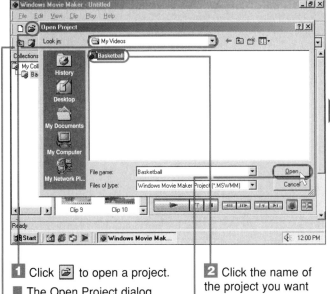

1 Click  to open a project.

■ The Open Project dialog
box appears.

■ This area shows the
location of the displayed
projects. You can click this
area to change the location.

2 Click the name of
the project you want
to open.

3 Click **Open** to
open the project.

■ The project opens
and the video clips in
the project appear on
the storyboard. You can
now review and make
changes to the video
clips on the storyboard.

■ You may need to use the
scroll bar to view the video
clips on the storyboard.

PREVIEW A MOVIE

You can preview all the video clips you added to the storyboard as a movie.

PREVIEW A MOVIE

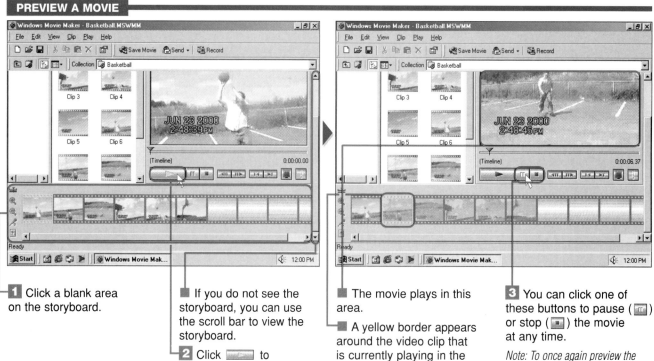

1 Click a blank area on the storyboard.

■ If you do not see the storyboard, you can use the scroll bar to view the storyboard.

2 Click ▭ to preview all the video clips you added to the storyboard as a movie.

■ The movie plays in this area.

■ A yellow border appears around the video clip that is currently playing in the movie.

3 You can click one of these buttons to pause (▭) or stop (▭) the movie at any time.

Note: To once again preview the movie, click ▭ .

When you finish using Windows Movie Maker, you can exit the program.

You should always exit Windows Movie Maker and all other programs before turning off your computer.

EXIT WINDOWS MOVIE MAKER

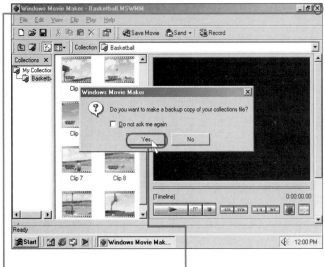

1 Click ☒ to exit Windows Movie Maker.

■ A dialog box may appear, asking if you want to make a backup copy of your collections file. Your collections file stores information about your video clips.

2 Click **Yes** to create a backup copy of your collections file.

Note: You can use the backup copy if the collections file is damaged or if you accidentally delete a collection or video clip.

■ The Collection Backup dialog box appears.

3 Type a name for the backup file.

■ This area shows the location where Windows Movie Maker will store the backup copy of the collections file. You can click this area to change the location.

4 Click **Save** to save the backup file.

SAVE A MOVIE

After you add all the video clips that you want to include in your movie to the storyboard, you can save the movie on your computer.

Saving a movie allows you to play the movie at any time and share the movie with friends and family.

SAVE A MOVIE

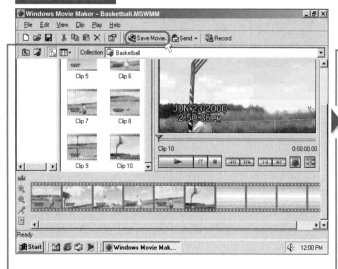

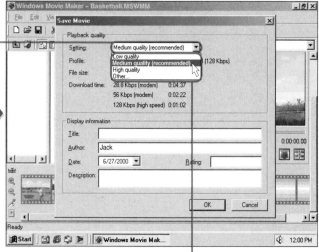

1 Click **Save Movie** to save the video clips on the storyboard as a movie.

■ The Save Movie dialog box appears.

2 Click this area to display a list of quality settings you can use for the movie.

3 Click the quality setting you want to use.

Note: Higher quality settings result in larger movie file sizes. Make sure you do not select a higher quality setting than you used to record your video.

How can I share a movie with friends and family?

John,

We are on vacation in Mexico, and we are having a wonderful time. The weather is fantastic and I am learning to water ski! Here is a short video that I've an attached file.

Mary

BIRD WATCHERS' HOME PAGE

The page dedicated to people who love to watch birds!

Send Movie in an E-mail Message

You can send a movie in an e-mail message to friends and family. You should try to keep your movies under 1 MB (or 1,000 KB). The computer receiving the message must have the necessary software to play the movie. To send a movie in an e-mail message, see page 282.

Add Movie to Web Page

You can add a movie to your Web page and then transfer the page to your Web server. A Web server is a computer on the Web that stores Web pages. Once the Web page is stored on your Web server, the movie will be available to everyone on the Web.

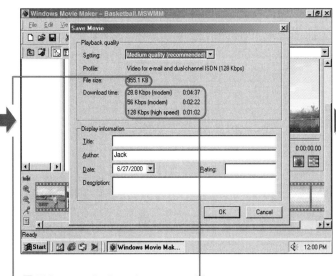

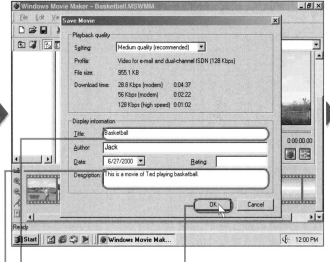

■ This area displays the file size of the movie.

■ This area displays the approximate amount of time the movie will take to transfer to another person's computer using three different types of Internet connections.

4 You can click this area and type a title for the movie.

5 You can click this area and type a description for the movie.

Note: The information you enter in steps 4 and 5 will be seen by people who view your movie in Windows Media Player.

6 Click **OK** to save the movie.

CONTINUED

SAVE A MOVIE

After you save a movie on your computer, you can view the movie in Windows Media Player.

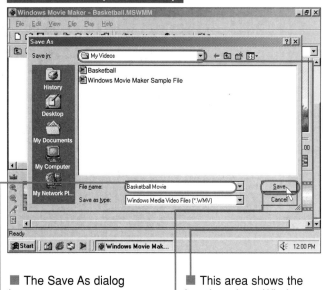

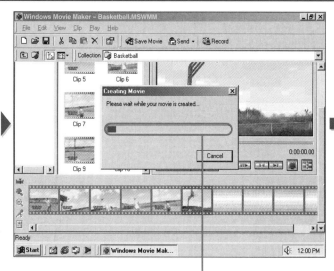

■ The Save As dialog box appears.

7 Type a name for the movie.

■ This area shows the location where Windows Movie Maker will store the movie. You can click this area to change the location.

8 Click **Save**.

■ The Creating Movie dialog box appears while Windows Movie Maker creates your movie.

■ This area shows the progress of the creation of the movie.

How can I later play a movie I have saved?

Windows automatically stores your movies in the My Videos folder on your computer. The My Videos folder is located within the My Documents folder on your desktop. To play a movie, double-click the movie in the My Videos folder.

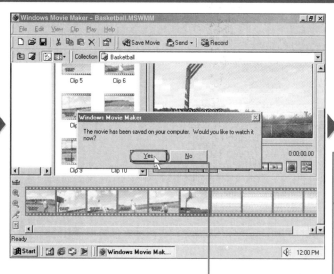

■ A dialog box appears when Windows Movie Maker has finished creating and saving your movie.

9 Click **Yes** to watch the movie now.

*Note: If you do not want to watch the movie now, click **No**.*

■ The Windows Media Player window appears.

■ The movie plays in this area.

10 You can click a button to pause ( ) or stop ( ) the movie at any time.

Note: The pause button changes to after you pause or stop the movie. To play the movie again, click .

11 When you finish viewing the movie, click ⊠ to close the Windows Media Player window.

CHAPTER 9

Optimize Your Computer

Discover several ways to enhance the overall performance of your computer. Learn how to install programs, schedule tasks, detect and repair disk errors, and obtain the latest Windows Me updates.

ADD WINDOWS COMPONENTS

You can add components to your computer that will add new programs and capabilities to Windows.

When installing Windows, most people do not install all the components that come with Windows. This prevents unneeded components from taking up storage space on your computer.

ADD WINDOWS COMPONENTS

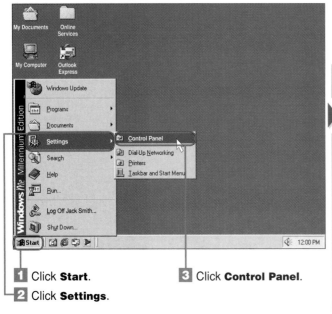

1 Click **Start**.

2 Click **Settings**.

3 Click **Control Panel**.

■ The Control Panel window appears.

4 Double-click **Add/Remove Programs**.

Note: The items in the Control Panel window may look different. If you do not see the Add/Remove Programs item, scroll through the window to display the item.

Which components can I add to my computer?

Windows offers many useful components that you
can add to your computer. Here are some examples.

Desktop Themes

Allows you to customize
the appearance of your
desktop using a particular
theme, such as a baseball
or jungle theme.

**Internet Connection
Sharing**

Allows multiple
computers to share
a single connection
to the Internet.

**Multimedia Sound
Schemes**

Provides sound effects
Windows can play when
you perform certain tasks
on your computer.

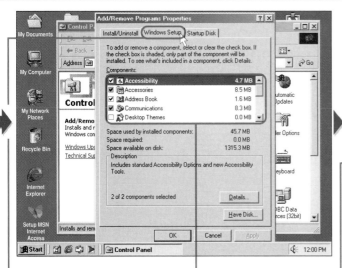

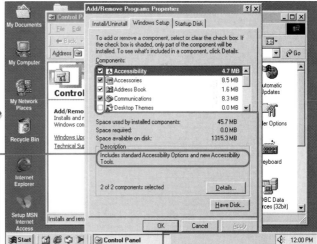

■ The Add/Remove
Programs Properties
dialog box appears.

5 Click the **Windows
Setup** tab.

■ This area displays the
categories of components
you can add to your
computer.

*Note: Windows may take a
moment to display the information.*

■ This area displays
a description of the
highlighted category.

*Note: You can click the
name of another category
to display its description.*

■ The box beside each
category indicates if all (☑),
some (☑) or none (☐) of the
components in the category are
installed on your computer.

CONTINUED

ADD WINDOWS COMPONENTS

You can view descriptions of Windows components to help you determine if you want to add the components to your computer.

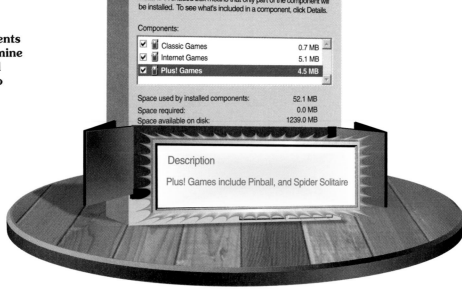

Games

To install a component, select the check box next to the component name, or clear the check box if you do not want to install it. A shaded box means that only part of the component will be installed. To see what's included in a component, click Details.

Components:

☑ Classic Games	0.7 MB
☑ Internet Games	5.1 MB
☑ **Plus! Games**	4.5 MB

Space used by installed components:	52.1 MB
Space required:	0.0 MB
Space available on disk:	1239.0 MB

Description

Plus! Games include Pinball, and Spider Solitaire

ADD WINDOWS COMPONENTS (CONTINUED)

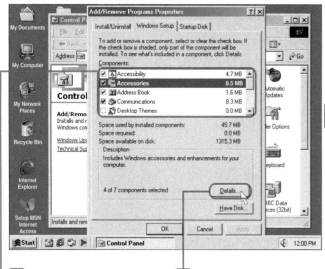

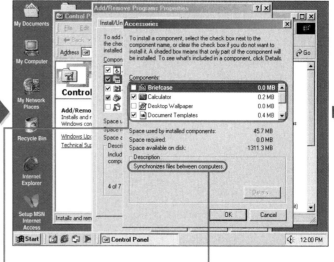

■6 Click the category that contains the component you want to add.

■7 Click **Details** to display the components in the category.

■ A dialog box appears.

■ This area displays the components in the category you selected.

■ This area displays a description of the highlighted component.

Note: You can click the name of another component to display its description.

How do I remove a component I do not use?

You can remove components you do not use to free up storage space on your computer. To remove a component you do not use, perform steps **1** to **11** starting on page 170. When you select a component you want to remove in step **8**, ✓ changes to ☐ .

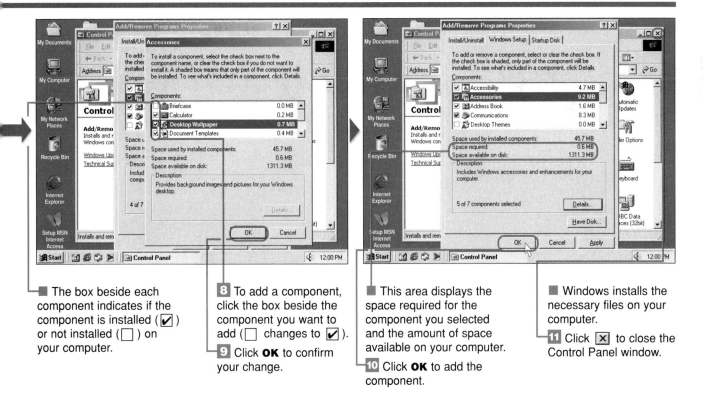

■ The box beside each component indicates if the component is installed (✓) or not installed (☐) on your computer.

8 To add a component, click the box beside the component you want to add (☐ changes to ✓).

9 Click **OK** to confirm your change.

■ This area displays the space required for the component you selected and the amount of space available on your computer.

10 Click **OK** to add the component.

■ Windows installs the necessary files on your computer.

11 Click ✗ to close the Control Panel window.

UPDATE WINDOWS

Windows can automatically update your computer with the latest Windows features available on the Internet.

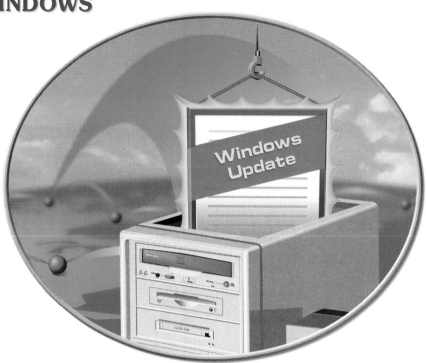

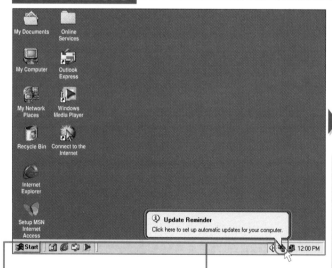

■ When you are connected to the Internet, this icon (🐾) and message appear when you can set up Windows to update your computer automatically.

1 Click the icon (🐾) to set up Windows to update your computer automatically.

■ The Updates wizard appears, stating that you can update your computer automatically by allowing Windows to search for important updates and information.

2 Click **Next** to continue.

How will Windows update my computer?

Windows can add new features to your computer and fix software problems to improve the performance of your computer. Windows will use the latest information available on the Internet to check for outdated software on your computer.

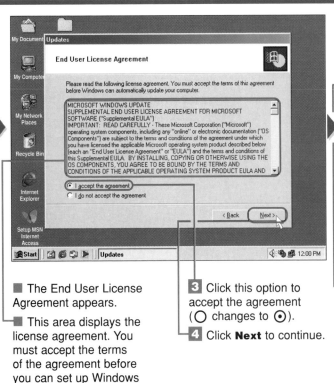

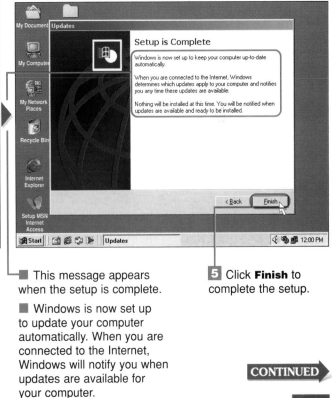

■ The End User License Agreement appears.

■ This area displays the license agreement. You must accept the terms of the agreement before you can set up Windows to update your computer automatically.

3 Click this option to accept the agreement (○ changes to ⊙).

4 Click **Next** to continue.

■ This message appears when the setup is complete.

■ Windows is now set up to update your computer automatically. When you are connected to the Internet, Windows will notify you when updates are available for your computer.

5 Click **Finish** to complete the setup.

CONTINUED

UPDATE WINDOWS

Windows will automatically determine which updates on the Internet apply to your computer and will notify you when the updates are available.

Windows will check for updates only when you are connected to the Internet.

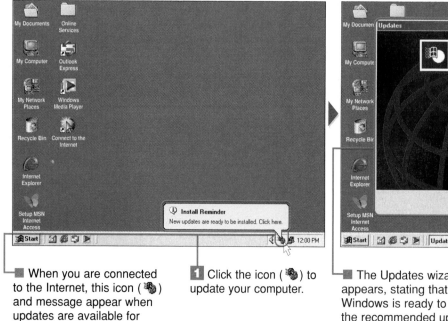

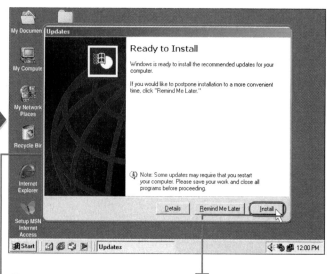

■ When you are connected to the Internet, this icon (🌏) and message appear when updates are available for your computer.

1 Click the icon (🌏) to update your computer.

■ The Updates wizard appears, stating that Windows is ready to install the recommended updates for your computer.

2 Click **Install** to install the updates.

Is there another way that I can update Windows?

You can also update Windows by using the Windows Update feature. This feature takes you to a Web site that can optimize the performance of your computer. The Web site can scan your computer and then determine a list of features that you can install to update Windows. To use the Windows Update feature, perform the following steps.

■ **1** Click **Start**.

■ **2** Click **Windows Update**.

■ If you are not connected to the Internet, a dialog box will appear, asking you to connect.

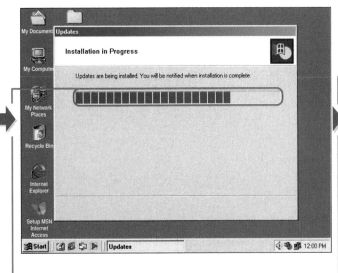

■ This area shows the progress of the installation.

■ This message appears if you need to restart your computer to complete the installation. Before restarting your computer, make sure you save your work and close any open programs.

■ **3** Click **Restart** to restart your computer.

*Note: If the "Installation Complete" message appears instead of the "Restart Needed" message, you do not need to restart your computer. Click **OK** instead of **Restart** in step 3 to complete the installation.*

INSTALL A PROGRAM

You can install a new program on your computer. Programs are available on CD-ROM discs and floppy disks.

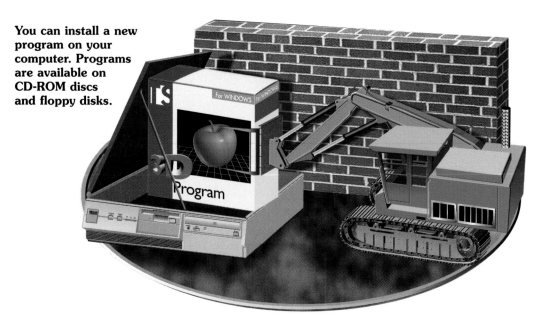

After you install a new program, make sure you keep the program's CD-ROM disc or floppy disks in a safe place. If your computer fails or you accidentally erase the program files, you may need to install the program again.

INSTALL A PROGRAM

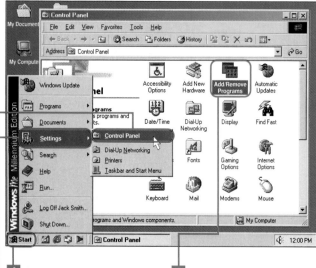

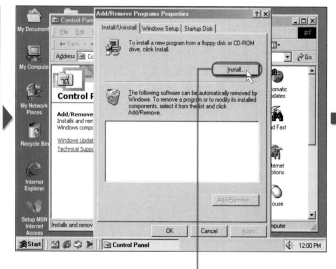

1 Click **Start**.

2 Click **Settings**.

3 Click **Control Panel**.

■ The Control Panel window appears.

4 Double-click **Add/Remove Programs**.

Note: The items in the Control Panel window may look different. If you do not see the Add/Remove Programs item, scroll through the window to display the item.

■ The Add/Remove Programs Properties dialog box appears.

5 Click **Install** to install a new program.

178

Why did an installation program appear when I inserted a program's CD-ROM disc into a drive on my computer?

Most programs available on a CD-ROM disc will automatically display an installation program when you insert the disc into a drive on your computer. Follow the instructions on your screen to install the program.

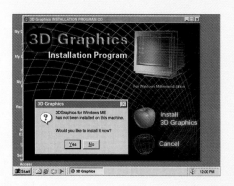

How can I install a program?

There are three common ways to install a program.

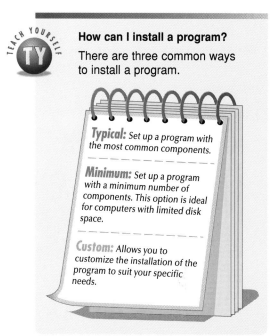

Typical: Set up a program with the most common components.

Minimum: Set up a program with a minimum number of components. This option is ideal for computers with limited disk space.

Custom: Allows you to customize the installation of the program to suit your specific needs.

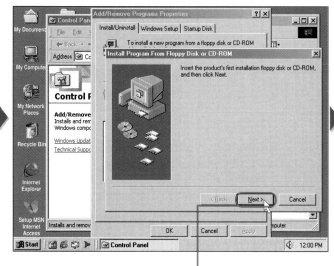

■ The Install Program From Floppy Disk or CD-ROM dialog box appears.

6 Insert the program's first installation floppy disk or CD-ROM disc into the appropriate drive on your computer.

7 Click **Next** to continue.

■ Windows locates the file needed to install the program.

8 Click **Finish** to install the program.

9 Follow the instructions on your screen. Every program will ask you a different set of questions.

REMOVE A PROGRAM

You can remove a program that you no longer use on your computer. Removing a program will free up space on your hard disk.

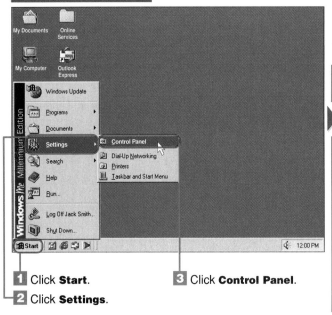

1 Click **Start**.

2 Click **Settings**.

3 Click **Control Panel**.

■ The Control Panel window appears.

4 Double-click **Add/Remove Programs** to remove a program from your computer.

Note: The items in the Control Panel window may look different. If you do not see the Add/Remove Programs item, scroll through the window to display the item.

Why doesn't the program I want to remove appear in the list of programs Windows can remove?

You can only use the method shown below to remove programs designed for Windows. For non-Windows programs, check the documentation supplied with the program to determine how to remove the program's files from your computer.

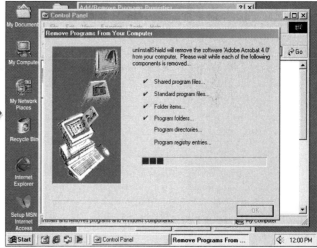

■ The Add/Remove Programs Properties dialog box appears.

■ This area lists the programs Windows can remove from your computer.

5 Click the program you want to remove.

6 Click **Add/Remove**.

■ Windows begins the process of removing the program from your computer.

7 Follow the instructions on your screen. Every program will take you through different steps to remove the program.

INSTALL A PRINTER

Before you can use a new printer, you need to install the printer on your computer. You only need to install a printer once.

Windows includes a wizard that guides you step by step through the process of installing a new printer.

INSTALL A PRINTER

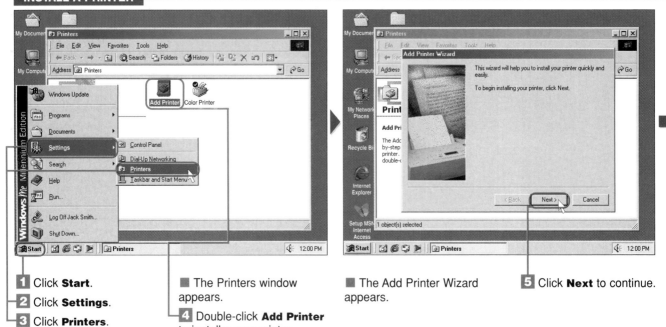

1 Click **Start**.

2 Click **Settings**.

3 Click **Printers**.

■ The Printers window appears.

4 Double-click **Add Printer** to install a new printer.

■ The Add Printer Wizard appears.

5 Click **Next** to continue.

What if the printer I want to install does not appear in the list?

If the printer you want to install does not appear in the list of printers in step **9** below, you can use the installation disk that came with your printer.

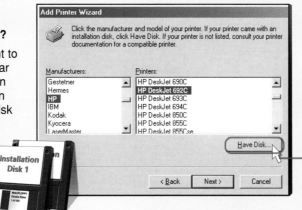

1 Insert the installation disk into a drive on your computer.

2 Click **Have Disk** and then press the Enter key.

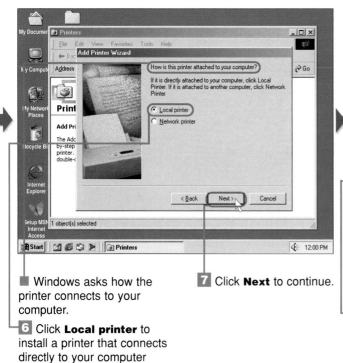

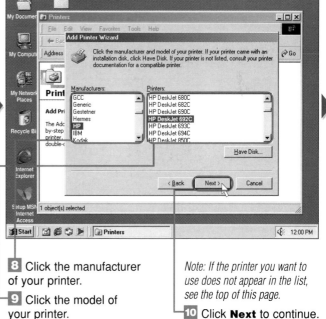

■ Windows asks how the printer connects to your computer.

6 Click **Local printer** to install a printer that connects directly to your computer (○ changes to ◉).

7 Click **Next** to continue.

8 Click the manufacturer of your printer.

9 Click the model of your printer.

Note: If the printer you want to use does not appear in the list, see the top of this page.

10 Click **Next** to continue.

CONTINUED

INSTALL A PRINTER

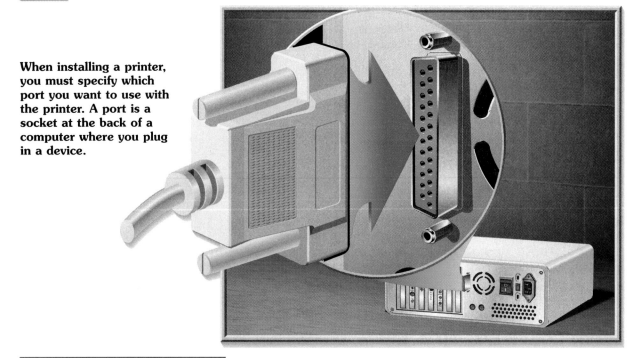

When installing a printer, you must specify which port you want to use with the printer. A port is a socket at the back of a computer where you plug in a device.

INSTALL A PRINTER (CONTINUED)

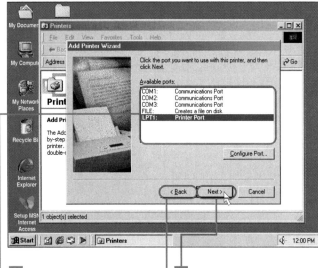

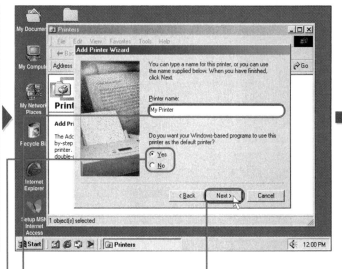

11 Click the port you want to use with the printer.

Note: LPT1 is the most commonly used port for printers.

12 Click **Next** to continue.

■ You can click **Back** at any time to return to a previous step and change your selections.

13 Windows provides a name for your printer. To use a different name, type a new name.

14 Click **Yes** or **No** to specify if you want to use the printer as your default printer (○ changes to ⊙). Files will automatically print to the default printer.

Note: If you are installing your first printer, you will not need to perform step 14.

15 Click **Next** to continue.

184

What is a Plug and Play printer?

A Plug and Play printer is a printer that Windows can automatically detect after you plug in the printer and turn on your computer. Windows will display the Add New Hardware Wizard to help you install the new printer. Follow the instructions on your screen to install the printer.

Why do I need to install a printer?

Installing a printer allows you to specify the printer driver Windows should use for the printer. A printer driver is special software that enables Windows to communicate with your printer. When you install a printer, Windows helps you select the correct printer driver for your printer.

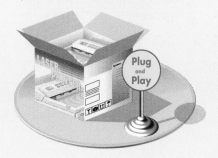

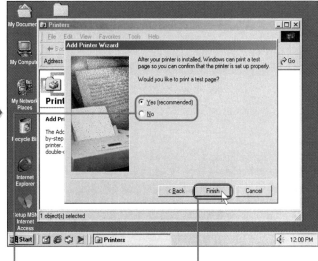

16 Click **Yes** or **No** to specify if you want to print a test page (○ changes to ⊙). A test page will confirm that your printer is set up properly.

17 Click **Finish** to install the printer.

■ An icon for the printer appears in the Printers window.

■ The printer displays a check mark (✓) if you chose to make the printer the default printer in step **14**.

Note: If you chose to print a test page in step 16, a dialog box will appear to confirm the test page printed correctly. Click Yes if the page printed correctly.

18 Click ☒ to close the Printers window.

INSTALL A PRINTER ON A NETWORK

Before you can use a printer attached to another computer on your network, you need to install the printer on your computer. You only need to install a printer once.

Before you can install a printer, the person who owns the computer attached to the printer must share the printer. To share a printer on a network, see page 232.

INSTALL A PRINTER ON A NETWORK

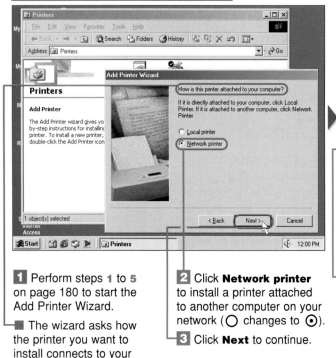

1 Perform steps **1** to **5** on page 180 to start the Add Printer Wizard.

■ The wizard asks how the printer you want to install connects to your computer.

2 Click **Network printer** to install a printer attached to another computer on your network (○ changes to ⊙).

3 Click **Next** to continue.

4 Click **Browse** to specify the location of the printer on your network that you want to install.

What do the icons in the Browse for Printer dialog box represent?

Each item in the Browse for Printer dialog box displays an icon to help you distinguish between the different types of items.

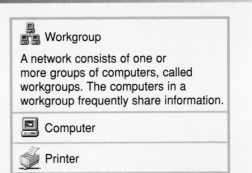

Workgroup

A network consists of one or more groups of computers, called workgroups. The computers in a workgroup frequently share information.

Computer

Printer

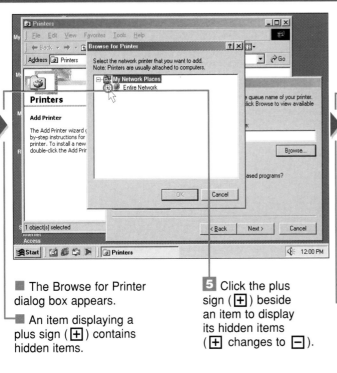

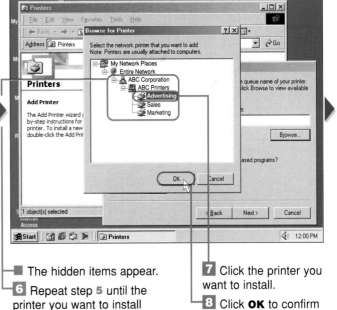

■ The Browse for Printer dialog box appears.

■ An item displaying a plus sign (⊞) contains hidden items.

5 Click the plus sign (⊞) beside an item to display its hidden items (⊞ changes to ⊟).

■ The hidden items appear.

6 Repeat step **5** until the printer you want to install appears. Printers display the 🖨 icon.

Note: For more information on the icons shown in the dialog box, see the top of this page.

7 Click the printer you want to install.

8 Click **OK** to confirm your selection.

CONTINUED

INSTALL A PRINTER ON A NETWORK

When installing a printer on your network, you can specify the name you want to use for the printer.

Specify Printer Name

Dan's Office

You may want to use a name for the printer that defines the location of the printer, such as "Dan's Office."

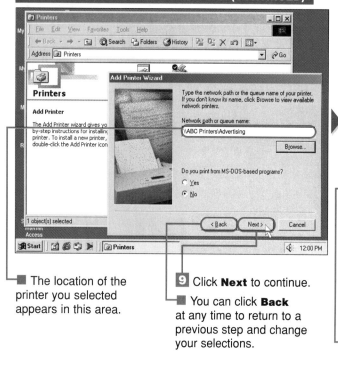

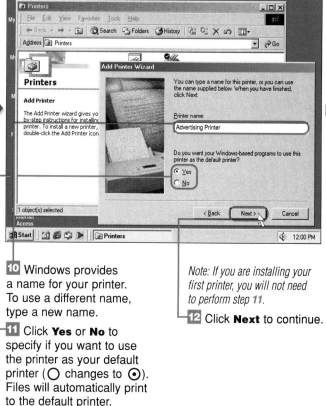

■ The location of the printer you selected appears in this area.

9 Click **Next** to continue.

■ You can click **Back** at any time to return to a previous step and change your selections.

10 Windows provides a name for your printer. To use a different name, type a new name.

11 Click **Yes** or **No** to specify if you want to use the printer as your default printer (○ changes to ◉). Files will automatically print to the default printer.

Note: If you are installing your first printer, you will not need to perform step 11.

12 Click **Next** to continue.

188

What is a dedicated network printer?

Many companies set up a computer and printer on a network whose only function is to print documents for people on the network. This type of printer is known as a dedicated network printer. A dedicated network printer can be placed in a central part of an office to make the printer easy to access. Companies can obtain dedicated network printers that have additional capabilities that are not available on standard printers, such as a job-sorting feature that organizes documents printed by many people.

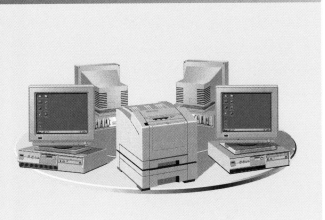

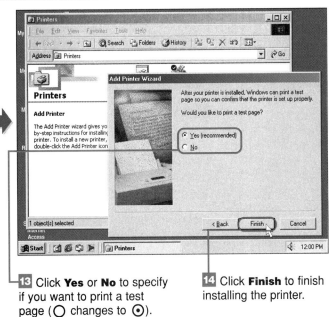

13 Click **Yes** or **No** to specify if you want to print a test page (○ changes to ⊙). A test page will confirm that the printer is set up properly.

14 Click **Finish** to finish installing the printer.

■ An icon for the printer appears in the Printers window.

■ The printer displays a check mark (✅) if you chose to make the printer the default printer in step **11**.

Note: If you chose to print a test page in step 13, a dialog box will appear to confirm the test page printed correctly. Click Yes if the page printed correctly.

15 Click ✗ to close the Printers window.

FORMAT A FLOPPY DISK

You must format a floppy disk before you can use the disk to store information.

Floppy disks you buy at computer stores are usually formatted. You may want to later format a floppy disk to erase the information it contains and prepare the disk for storing new information.

FORMAT A FLOPPY DISK

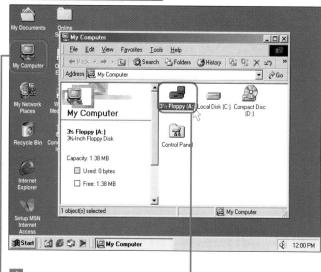

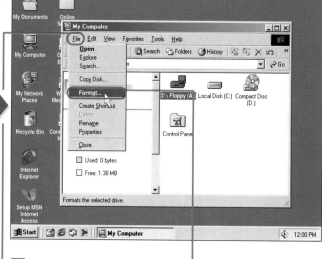

1 Insert the floppy disk you want to format into your floppy drive.

2 Double-click **My Computer**.

■ The My Computer window appears.

3 Click the drive that contains the floppy disk you want to format.

4 Click **File**.

5 Click **Format**.

How can I tell how much information a floppy disk can store?

Double-Density Floppy Disk

A 3.5-inch floppy disk that has one hole can store 720 KB of information.

High-Density Floppy Disk

A 3.5-inch floppy disk that has two holes and displays the HD symbol can store 1.44 MB of information.

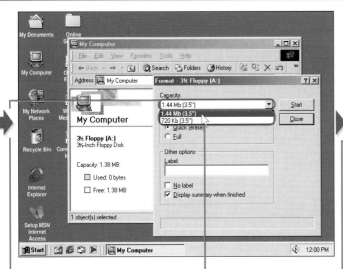

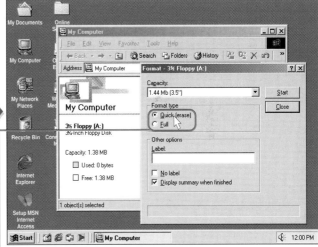

■ The Format dialog box appears.

6 Click this area to specify how much information the floppy disk can store.

7 Click the storage capacity of the floppy disk.

Note: For more information, see the top of this page.

8 Click the type of format you want to perform (○ changes to ⊙).

*Note: If the floppy disk has never been formatted, select the **Full** option.*

Quick (erase)

Removes all files but does not scan the disk for damaged areas.

Full

Removes all files and scans the disk for damaged areas.

FORMAT A FLOPPY DISK

Before formatting a floppy disk, make sure the disk does not contain information you may need. Formatting a floppy disk will permanently remove all the information on the disk.

MicroFLOPPY
Double Sided
1.44 MB

FORMAT A FLOPPY DISK (CONTINUED)

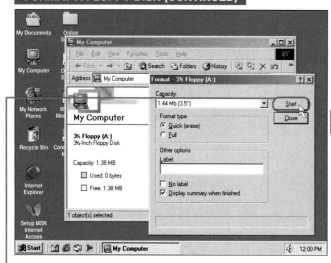

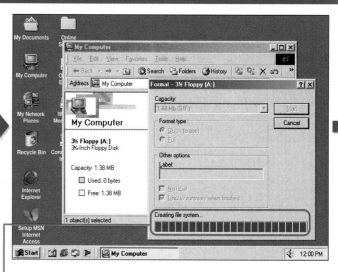

9 Click **Start** to start formatting the floppy disk.

■ This area displays the progress of the format.

192

How can I tell if a floppy disk is formatted?

Windows will display an error message when you try to view the contents of a floppy disk that is not formatted. You cannot tell if a floppy disk is formatted just by looking at the disk. To view the contents of a floppy disk, see page 48.

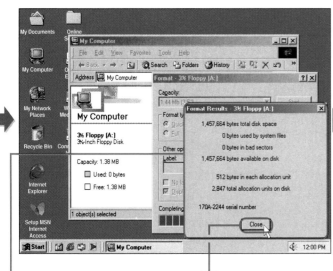

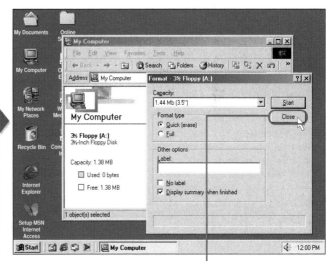

■ The Format Results dialog box appears when the format is complete. The dialog box displays information about the formatted disk, such as the total disk space.

10 When you finish reviewing the information, click **Close** to close the dialog box.

■ To format another floppy disk, insert the disk and then repeat steps **6** to **10** starting on page 191.

11 Click **Close** to close the Format dialog box.

VIEW AMOUNT OF DISK SPACE

You can view the amount of used and free space on a disk.

You should check the amount of free space on your computer's hard disk (C:) at least once a month. You should have at least 10% of your total hard disk space free.

VIEW AMOUNT OF DISK SPACE

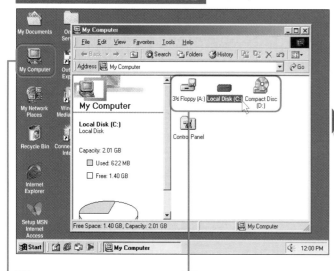

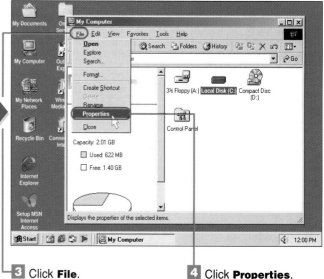

1 Double-click **My Computer**.

■ The My Computer window appears.

2 To view the amount of space on a disk, click the disk of interest.

Note: To view the amount of space on a floppy disk, you must insert the disk into the floppy drive before performing step 2.

3 Click **File**.

4 Click **Properties**.

How can I increase the amount of free space on my hard disk?

Delete Files

Delete files you no longer need from your computer. To delete files, see page 72.

Use Disk Cleanup

Use Disk Cleanup to remove unnecessary files from your computer. To use Disk Cleanup, see page 200.

Remove Programs

Remove programs you no longer use from your computer. To remove programs, see page 180.

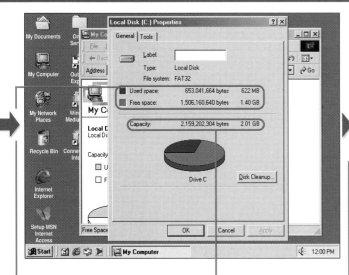

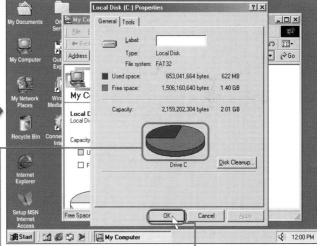

■ The Properties dialog box appears.

■ This area displays the amount of used and free space on the disk in bytes, megabytes (MB) and gigabytes (GB).

■ This area displays the total disk storage space, in both bytes and gigabytes (GB).

■ This pie chart displays the amount of used and free space on the disk.

5 When you finish reviewing the information, click **OK** to close the Properties dialog box.

DEFRAGMENT YOUR HARD DISK

You can improve the performance of your computer by defragmenting your hard disk.

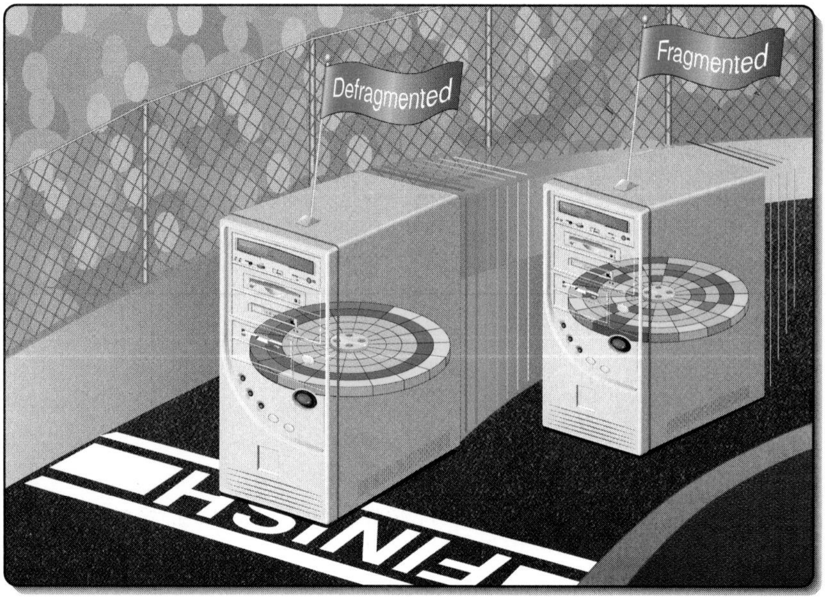

The hard disk is the primary device a computer uses to store information. You should defragment your hard disk at least once a month.

DEFRAGMENT YOUR HARD DISK

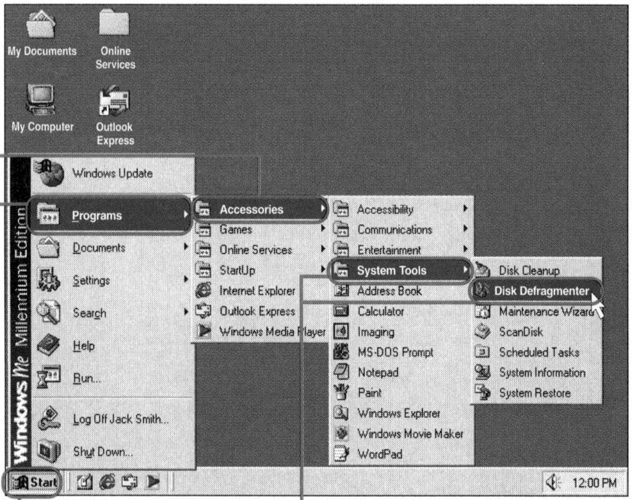

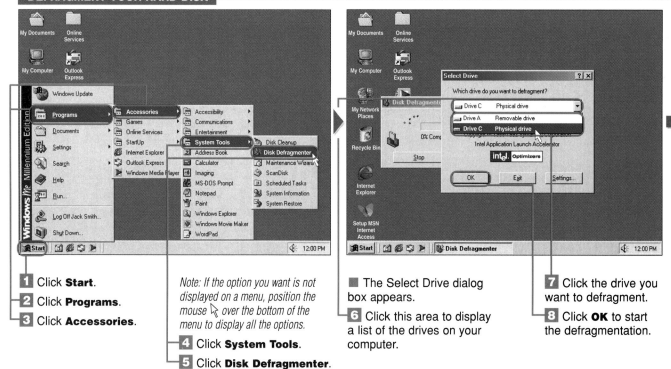

1 Click **Start**.

2 Click **Programs**.

3 Click **Accessories**.

Note: If the option you want is not displayed on a menu, position the mouse over the bottom of the menu to display all the options.

4 Click **System Tools**.

5 Click **Disk Defragmenter**.

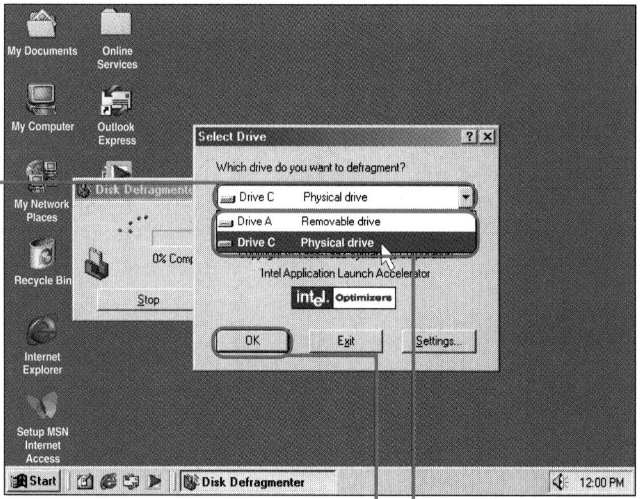

■ The Select Drive dialog box appears.

6 Click this area to display a list of the drives on your computer.

7 Click the drive you want to defragment.

8 Click **OK** to start the defragmentation.

Why would I need to defragment my hard disk?

A fragmented hard disk stores parts of a file in many different locations on the disk. Your computer must search many areas on the disk to retrieve a file. You can use Disk Defragmenter to place all the parts of a file in one location. This reduces the time your computer will spend locating files.

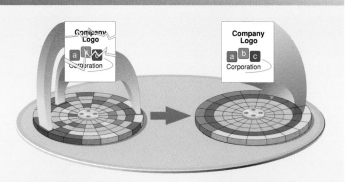

**Fragmented
Hard Disk**

**Defragmented
Hard Disk**

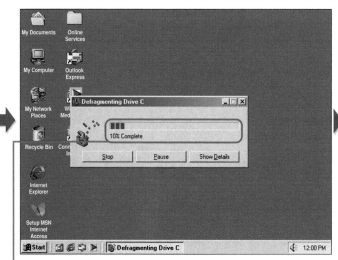

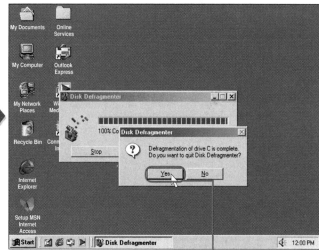

■ The Defragmenting Drive window appears.

■ This area displays the progress of the defragmentation.

Note: You should try to avoid performing other tasks on your computer during the defragmentation. If you perform other tasks during the defragmentation, your computer will operate more slowly and the defragmentation will take longer or may restart.

■ A dialog box appears when the defragmentation of the hard disk is complete.

9 Click **Yes** to close Disk Defragmenter.

DETECT AND REPAIR DISK ERRORS

You can improve the performance of your computer by using ScanDisk to detect and repair hard disk errors.

The hard disk is the primary device a computer uses to store information. You should check your hard disk for errors at least once a month.

DETECT AND REPAIR DISK ERRORS

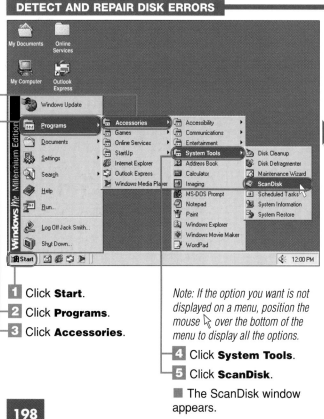

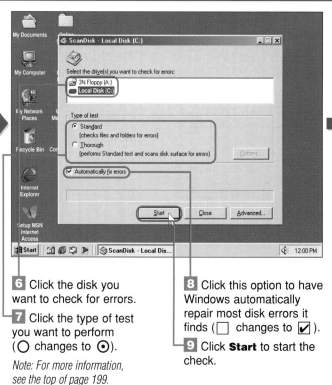

1 Click **Start**.

2 Click **Programs**.

3 Click **Accessories**.

Note: If the option you want is not displayed on a menu, position the mouse ⓚ over the bottom of the menu to display all the options.

4 Click **System Tools**.

5 Click **ScanDisk**.

■ The ScanDisk window appears.

6 Click the disk you want to check for errors.

7 Click the type of test you want to perform (○ changes to ⊙).

Note: For more information, see the top of page 199.

8 Click this option to have Windows automatically repair most disk errors it finds (☐ changes to ☑).

9 Click **Start** to start the check.

198

What type of test can I perform on my hard disk?

Standard

The Standard test checks the files and folders on the disk for errors.

Thorough

The Thorough test checks the files and folders on the disk as well as the surface of the disk for errors.

Windows will automatically perform the Standard test if you did not properly shut down Windows the last time you used the program. For example, the Standard test will run if your computer temporarily lost power.

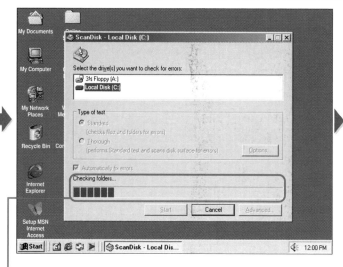

■ This area displays the progress of the check.

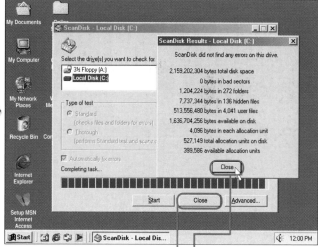

■ The ScanDisk Results dialog box appears when the check is complete. The dialog box displays information about the disk, such as the total disk space.

10 When you finish reviewing the information, click **Close** to close the dialog box.

11 Click **Close** to close the ScanDisk window.

You can use Disk
Cleanup to remove
unnecessary files
from your computer
and free up disk
space.

USING DISK CLEANUP

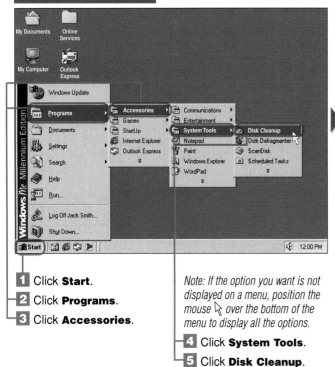

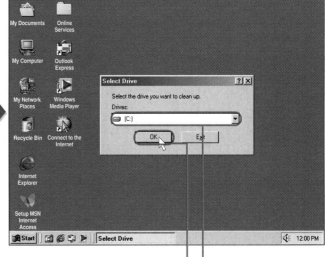

1 Click **Start**.

2 Click **Programs**.

3 Click **Accessories**.

Note: If the option you want is not displayed on a menu, position the mouse ⊢ over the bottom of the menu to display all the options.

4 Click **System Tools**.

5 Click **Disk Cleanup**.

■ The Select Drive dialog box appears.

■ This area displays the drive that Windows will clean up. You can click this area to select a different drive.

6 Click **OK**.

What types of files can Disk Cleanup remove?

File Type	Description
Temporary Internet Files	Web pages stored on your computer for quick viewing.
Downloaded Program Files	Program files transferred automatically from the Internet and stored on your computer when you view certain Web pages.
Recycle Bin	Files you have deleted.
Temporary Files	Files created by programs to store temporary information.
Temporary PC Health Files	Files the PC Health program can use to ensure your computer operates smoothly.

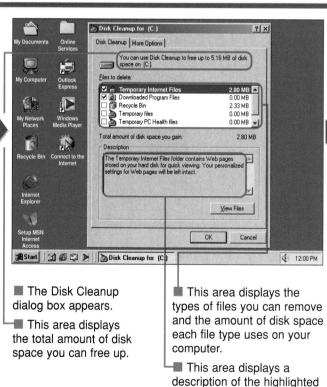

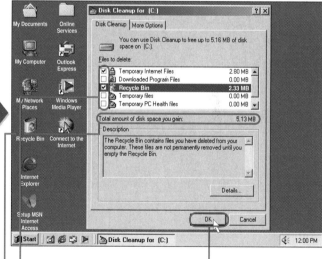

■ The Disk Cleanup dialog box appears.

■ This area displays the total amount of disk space you can free up.

■ This area displays the types of files you can remove and the amount of disk space each file type uses on your computer.

■ This area displays a description of the highlighted file type.

7 Windows will remove the files for each file type that displays a check mark (☑). You can click the box (☐) beside a file type to add or remove the check mark.

■ This area displays the total disk space Windows will free up by deleting the file types you selected.

8 Click **OK** to remove the files.

■ A confirmation dialog box appears. Click **Yes** to permanently delete the files.

SCHEDULE TASKS

You can use
Task Scheduler
to have Windows
automatically
run specific
programs on a
regular basis.

Using Task Scheduler
is ideal for running
computer maintenance
programs such as Disk
Cleanup and ScanDisk.

SCHEDULE TASKS

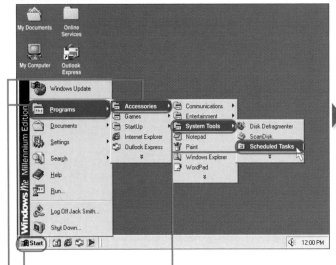

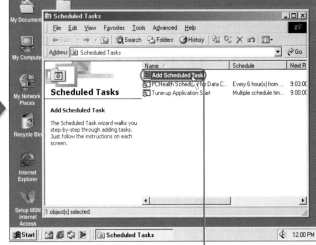

1 Click **Start**.

2 Click **Programs**.

3 Click **Accessories**.

*Note: If the option you want is not
displayed on a menu, position the
mouse ⟨ over the bottom of the
menu to display all the options.*

4 Click **System Tools**.

5 Click **Scheduled Tasks**.

■ The Scheduled Tasks
window appears.

6 Double-click **Add
Scheduled Task** to
schedule a program.

How does Task Scheduler know when to start a program?

Task Scheduler uses the date and time set in your computer to determine when to start a scheduled program. You should make sure the date and time set in your computer is correct before you schedule a program. To change the date and time set in your computer, see page 100.

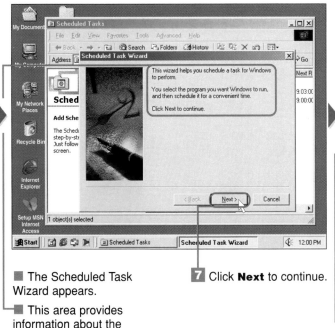

■ The Scheduled Task Wizard appears.

■ This area provides information about the wizard.

7 Click **Next** to continue.

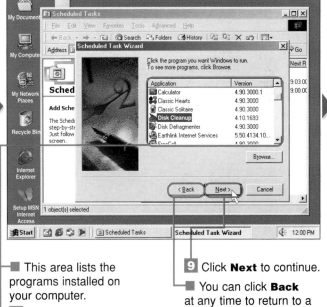

■ This area lists the programs installed on your computer.

8 Click the program you want Windows to run automatically.

9 Click **Next** to continue.

■ You can click **Back** at any time to return to a previous step and change your choices.

CONTINUED

SCHEDULE TASKS

You can specify
the date and
time you want
Task Scheduler
to start a
program.

Make sure you
schedule a program
for a time when
your computer will
be turned on.

SCHEDULE TASKS (CONTINUED)

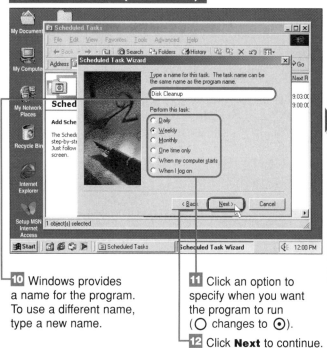

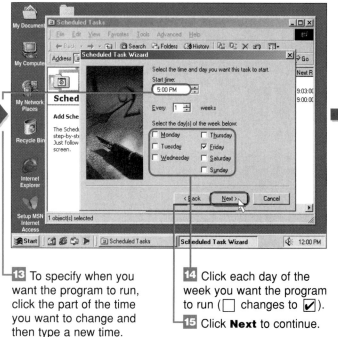

10 Windows provides
a name for the program.
To use a different name,
type a new name.

11 Click an option to
specify when you want
the program to run
(○ changes to ⊙).

12 Click **Next** to continue.

13 To specify when you
want the program to run,
click the part of the time
you want to change and
then type a new time.

*Note: The options available
in this screen depend on the
option you selected in step 11.*

14 Click each day of the
week you want the program
to run (☐ changes to ☑).

15 Click **Next** to continue.

How do I stop Windows from running a program automatically?

To stop Windows from running a program automatically, you must remove the program from the Scheduled Tasks window.

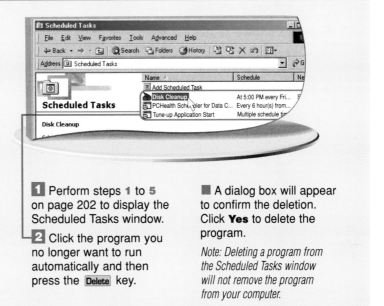

1 Perform steps **1** to **5** on page 202 to display the Scheduled Tasks window.

2 Click the program you no longer want to run automatically and then press the Delete key.

■ A dialog box will appear to confirm the deletion. Click **Yes** to delete the program.

Note: Deleting a program from the Scheduled Tasks window will not remove the program from your computer.

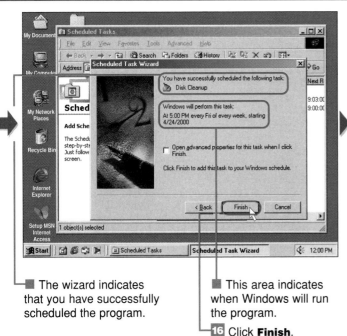

■ The wizard indicates that you have successfully scheduled the program.

■ This area indicates when Windows will run the program.

16 Click **Finish**.

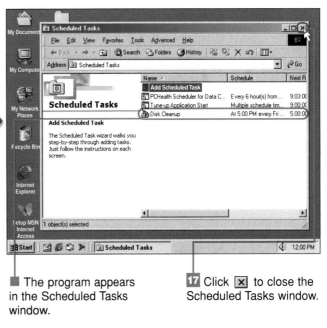

■ The program appears in the Scheduled Tasks window.

17 Click ⊠ to close the Scheduled Tasks window.

USING THE MAINTENANCE WIZARD

You can use the Maintenance Wizard to schedule regular maintenance tasks to optimize the performance of your computer.

USING THE MAINTENANCE WIZARD

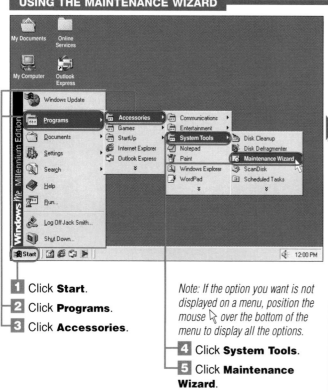

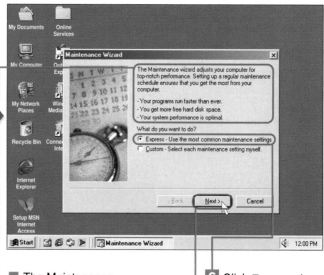

1 Click **Start**.

2 Click **Programs**.

3 Click **Accessories**.

Note: If the option you want is not displayed on a menu, position the mouse ⬚ over the bottom of the menu to display all the options.

4 Click **System Tools**.

5 Click **Maintenance Wizard**.

■ The Maintenance Wizard appears.

Note: A different dialog box appears if you have previously used the Maintenance Wizard. To change the Maintenance Wizard settings, see page 209.

■ This area describes the Maintenance Wizard.

6 Click **Express** to use the most common maintenance settings (○ changes to ⊙).

7 Click **Next** to continue.

206

What tasks does the Maintenance Wizard perform?

Disk Defragmenter

Runs Disk Defragmenter to speed up your programs. For more information on Disk Defragmenter, see page 196.

ScanDisk

Runs ScanDisk to check your hard disk for errors. For more information on ScanDisk, see page 198.

Disk Cleanup

Runs Disk Cleanup to delete unnecessary files from your computer to free up disk space. For more information on Disk Cleanup, see page 200.

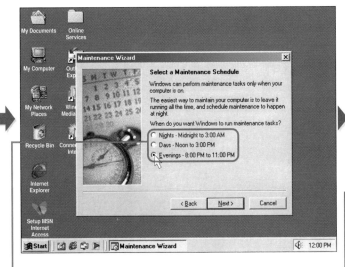

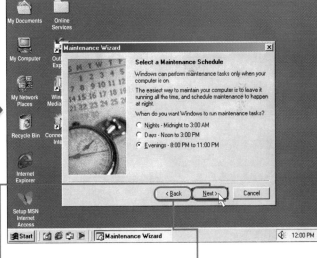

8 Click an option to select when you want to schedule your maintenance tasks (○ changes to ⊙).

Note: You should schedule maintenance tasks to run when your computer will be turned on.

9 Click **Next** to continue.

■ You can click **Back** at any time to return to a previous step and change your selections.

CONTINUED

USING THE MAINTENANCE WIZARD

After you use the Maintenance Wizard to schedule maintenance tasks, make sure your computer is turned on when the tasks will run.

USING THE MAINTENANCE WIZARD (CONTINUED)

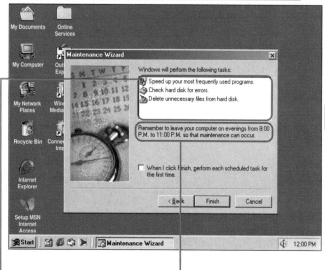

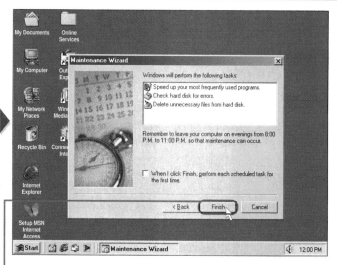

■ This area lists the maintenance tasks that Windows will perform.

■ This area indicates when the maintenance tasks will run. Make sure your computer is turned on during this time.

10 Click **Finish** to finish scheduling the maintenance tasks.

■ Windows will run the maintenance tasks at the scheduled time.

How does Windows know when to start scheduled maintenance tasks?

Windows uses the date and time set in your computer to determine when to start scheduled maintenance tasks. You should make sure the date and time set in your computer is correct before you schedule maintenance tasks. To change the date and time set in your computer, see page 100.

How do I stop Windows from running a scheduled maintenance task?

The Maintenance Wizard adds each maintenance task to the Scheduled Tasks window. To stop Windows from running a scheduled maintenance task, you must remove the task from the Scheduled Tasks window. To remove a task from the Scheduled Tasks window, see the top of page 205.

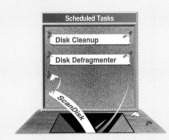

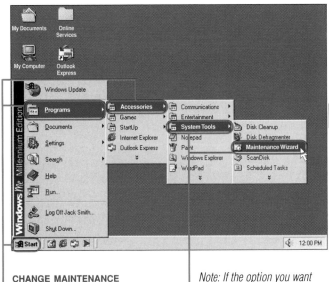

CHANGE MAINTENANCE SETTINGS

■1 Click **Start**.

■2 Click **Programs**.

■3 Click **Accessories**.

Note: If the option you want is not displayed on a menu, position the mouse ▷ over the bottom of the menu to display all the options.

■4 Click **System Tools**.

■5 Click **Maintenance Wizard**.

■ The Maintenance Wizard dialog box appears.

■6 Click this option to change your maintenance settings (○ changes to ⊙).

■7 Click **OK**.

■ The Maintenance Wizard appears.

■8 Perform steps **6** to **10** starting on page 206 to change your maintenance settings.

START A PROGRAM AUTOMATICALLY

If you use the
same program every
day, you can have
the program start
automatically each
time you turn on
your computer.

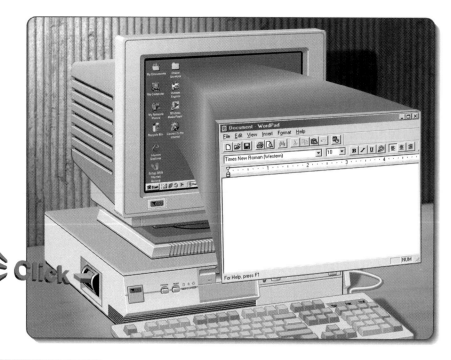

Click

START A PROGRAM AUTOMATICALLY

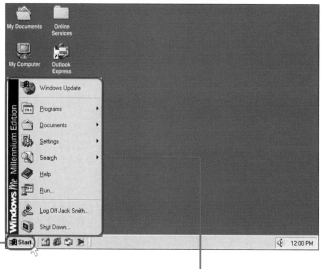

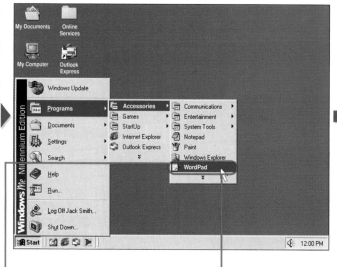

CREATE SHORTCUT PROGRAM

Before you can start a
program automatically, you
need to locate the program
on the Start menu.

1 Click **Start** to display
the Start menu.

■ The Start menu
appears.

2 Position the mouse �
over the program you want
to start automatically.

*Note: To use the Start menu,
see page 10.*

3 Right-click the
program you want
to start automatically.
A menu appears.

210

How can I display a list of all the programs that will start automatically?

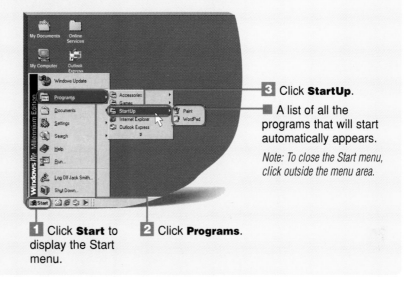

3 Click **StartUp**.

■ A list of all the programs that will start automatically appears.

Note: To close the Start menu, click outside the menu area.

1 Click **Start** to display the Start menu.

2 Click **Programs**.

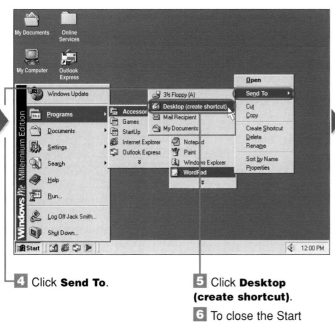

4 Click **Send To**.

5 Click **Desktop (create shortcut)**.

6 To close the Start menu, click outside the menu area.

■ A shortcut for the program appears on your desktop.

Note: For information on shortcuts, see page 86.

■ To start the program automatically, you need to add the shortcut for the program to the StartUp folder as shown on page 212.

CONTINUED

START A PROGRAM AUTOMATICALLY

You must add the
shortcut for the
program you want
to start automatically
to the StartUp folder.

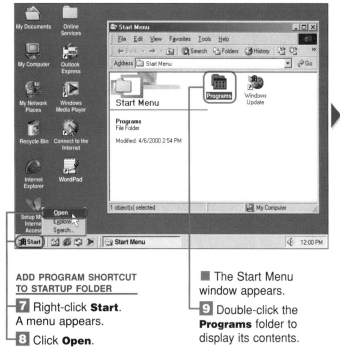

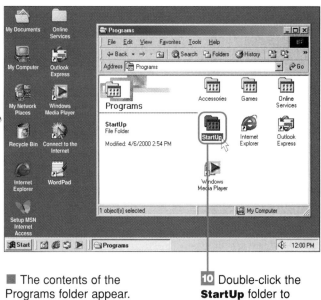

**ADD PROGRAM SHORTCUT
TO STARTUP FOLDER**

7 Right-click **Start**.
A menu appears.

8 Click **Open**.

■ The Start Menu
window appears.

9 Double-click the
Programs folder to
display its contents.

■ The contents of the
Programs folder appear.

10 Double-click the
StartUp folder to
display its contents.

How do I stop a program from starting automatically?

To stop a program from starting automatically, you must remove the shortcut for the program from the StartUp window.

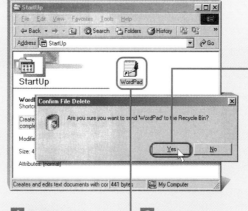

■ A dialog box will appear to confirm the deletion. Click **Yes** to delete the shortcut for the program.

Note: Deleting a shortcut for a program from the StartUp window will not remove the program from your computer.

1 Perform steps **7** to **10** below to display the StartUp window.

2 Click the shortcut for the program and then press the Delete key.

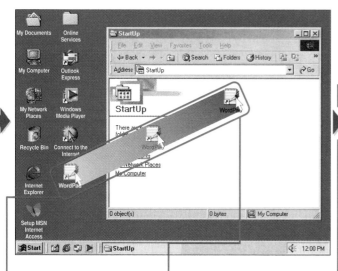

■ The contents of the StartUp folder appear.

11 Position the mouse over the shortcut for the program you added to the desktop.

Note: If you cannot see the shortcut for the program, you may need to move or resize the StartUp window. To move or resize a window, see pages 16 or 17.

12 Drag the shortcut to a blank area in the StartUp window.

■ Windows places the shortcut for the program in the StartUp window.

■ Each program in the StartUp window will start automatically each time you turn on your computer.

13 Click ✕ to close the StartUp window.

RESTORE YOUR COMPUTER

If you are experiencing problems with your computer, you can use the System Restore feature to return your computer to a time before the problems occurred.

For example, if you accidentally delete program files, you can restore your computer to a time before you deleted the files.

RESTORE YOUR COMPUTER

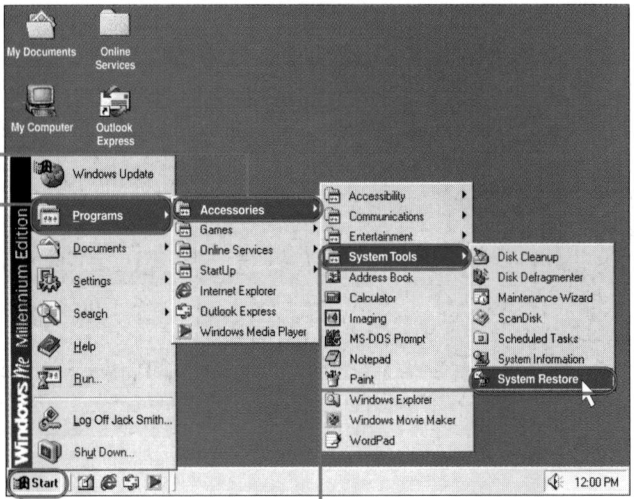

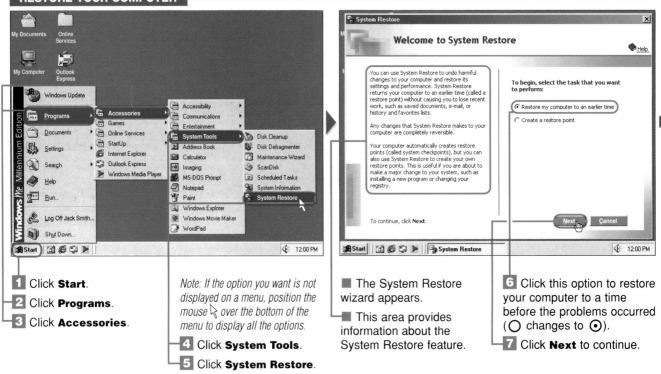

1. Click **Start**.
2. Click **Programs**.
3. Click **Accessories**.

Note: If the option you want is not displayed on a menu, position the mouse over the bottom of the menu to display all the options.

4. Click **System Tools**.
5. Click **System Restore**.

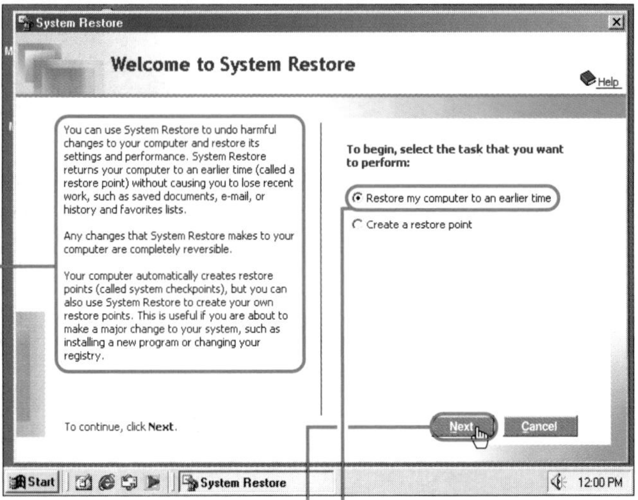

■ The System Restore wizard appears.

■ This area provides information about the System Restore feature.

6. Click this option to restore your computer to a time before the problems occurred (○ changes to ⊙).
7. Click **Next** to continue.

What types of restore points can I use?

You can return your computer to an earlier, more stable time, called a restore point. Windows can store between one to three weeks of restore points. Here are a few types of restore points:

System CheckPoint

Restore points created automatically by Windows on a regular basis.

Installed (Program)

Restore points created automatically when you install certain programs. The name of the program appears beside the word "Installed."

Windows Automatic Update Install

Restore points created when you install updates for Windows using the Windows Auto Update feature. To automatically update Windows, see page 174.

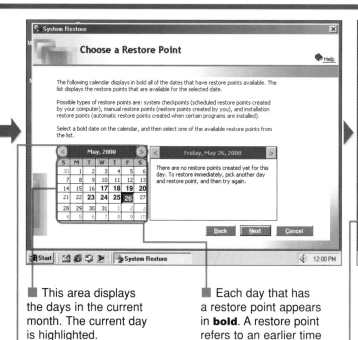

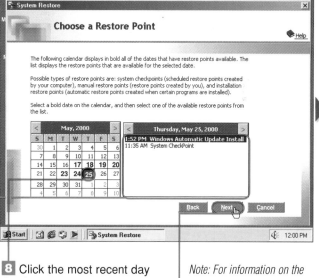

■ This area displays the days in the current month. The current day is highlighted.

■ You can click ◄ or ► to display the days in the previous or next month.

■ Each day that has a restore point appears in **bold**. A restore point refers to an earlier time that you can return your computer to.

8 Click the most recent day that has a restore point when your computer was working properly. The day is highlighted.

■ This area lists the restore points available for the day you selected.

9 Click the restore point you want to use.

Note: For information on the types of restore points you can use, see the top of this page.

10 Click **Next** to continue.

CONTINUED

RESTORE YOUR COMPUTER

Before restoring your computer to an earlier time, you should close all open files and programs.

When you restore your computer to an earlier time, you will not lose any work, such as e-mail messages or documents, that you worked with since that time.

RESTORE YOUR COMPUTER (CONTINUED)

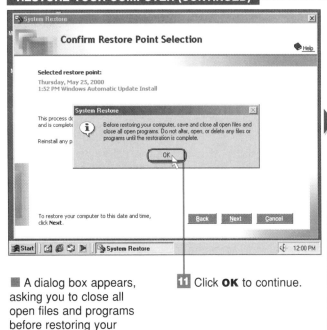

■ A dialog box appears, asking you to close all open files and programs before restoring your computer.

11 Click **OK** to continue.

■ This area displays information about the restore point you selected.

12 Click **Next** to continue.

■ You can click **Back** at any time to return to a previous screen and change your selections.

Will I need to reinstall any programs after restoring my computer?

When you restore your computer to an earlier time, any programs you installed after that date will be uninstalled. Files you created using the program will not be deleted, but you will need to reinstall the program to work with the files again.

Can I reverse the changes made when I restored my computer?

Yes. Any changes that System Restore makes to your computer are completely reversible. To undo the last restore, perform steps **1** to **7** on page 214, except select **Undo my last restoration** in step **6**. Then perform steps **11** to **13** below.

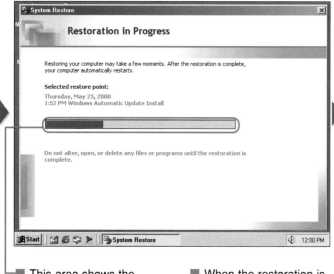

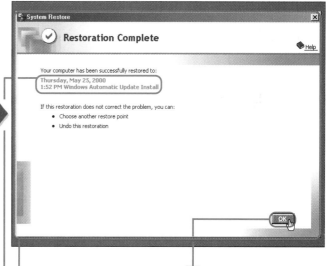

■ This area shows the progress of the restoration.

■ You should not work with any files or programs until the restoration is complete.

■ When the restoration is complete, your computer will automatically restart.

■ After your computer restarts, this message appears to indicate that the restoration of your computer is complete.

■ Windows has restored your computer to the date displayed in this area.

13 Click **OK** to close the System Restore wizard.

CHAPTER 10

Work on a Network

In this chapter you will learn how to set up and exchange information on a network, install a network protocol and much more.

TURN ON SHARING

Before you can share information or a printer with other people on a network, you must set up your computer to share resources.

TURN ON SHARING

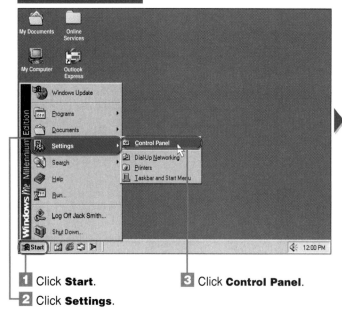

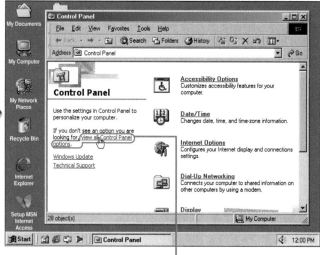

1 Click **Start**.

2 Click **Settings**.

3 Click **Control Panel**.

■ The Control Panel window appears.

4 If all the items do not appear in the Control Panel window, click **view all Control Panel options** to display all the items.

What is a network?

A network is a group of connected computers that allow people to share information and equipment.

Share Information

Networks allow people to easily share data and programs. You can exchange documents, spreadsheets, pictures and electronic mail between computers.

Share Equipment

Computers connected to a network can share equipment, such as a printer, to reduce costs. For example, rather than buying a printer for each person on a network, everyone can share one central printer.

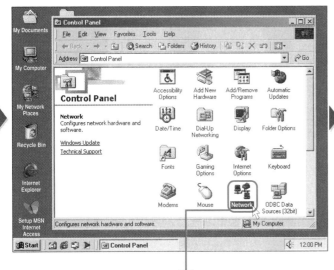

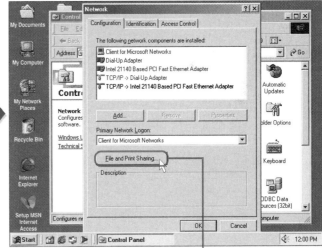

■ All of the items appear in the Control Panel window.

5 Double-click **Network** to change the network settings for your computer.

■ The Network dialog box appears.

6 Click **File and Print Sharing**.

CONTINUED ▶

TURN ON SHARING

Windows will ask you to restart your computer before you can share your files or printer with other people on the network.

Make sure you close any open programs before restarting your computer.

After you turn on sharing, new printers you install are automatically shared.

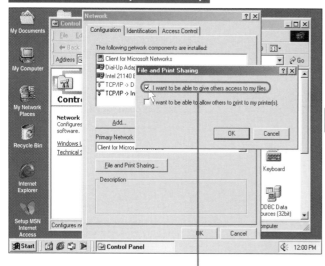

■ The File and Print Sharing dialog box appears.

7 Click this option to be able to share your files with other people on your network (☐ changes to ☑).

8 Click this option to be able to share your printer with other people on your network (☐ changes to ☑).

9 Click **OK** to confirm your selections.

I turned on sharing, but my colleagues still cannot access my files and printer. What is wrong?

Specify Files to Share

Once you turn on sharing, you must specify exactly what you want to share. To specify the folders that contain the files you want to share, see page 228. To specify the printer you want to share, see page 232.

Install a Network Protocol

To share files and a printer, you may need to install the network protocol used by your network to exchange information. A network protocol is a language, or a set of rules, that determines how computers on a network communicate. To install a network protocol, see page 224.

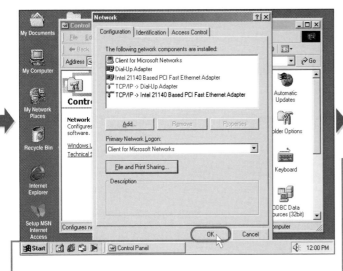

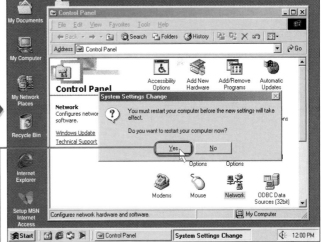

■ **10** Click **OK** to close the Network dialog box.

■ Windows sets up the necessary files on your computer.

■ The System Settings Change dialog box appears, stating that Windows needs to restart your computer before the new settings will take effect.

■ **11** Click **Yes** to restart your computer.

■ To later turn off sharing, perform steps **1** to **11** starting on page 220 (☑ changes to ☐ in steps **7** and **8**).

INSTALL A NETWORK PROTOCOL

You may need to install a network protocol on your computer to allow your computer to exchange information with other computers on a network.

When you first install Windows, some network protocols are automatically installed on your computer.

INSTALL A NETWORK PROTOCOL

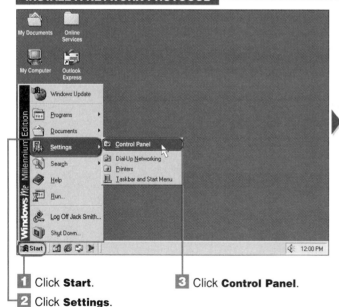

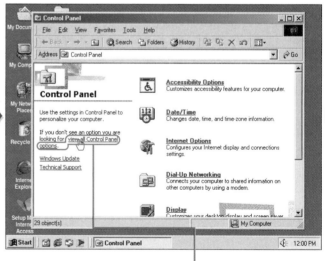

1 Click **Start**.

2 Click **Settings**.

3 Click **Control Panel**.

■ The Control Panel window appears.

4 If all the items do not appear in the Control Panel window, click **view all Control Panel options** to display all the items.

Why do I need to install a network protocol?

A network protocol is a language, or a set of rules, that determines how computers on a network communicate. All computers on a network must use the same network protocol to communicate with each other. A network protocol checks for errors when a computer transfers information over the network and can correct any errors by having the computer resend the information.

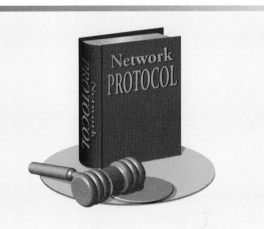

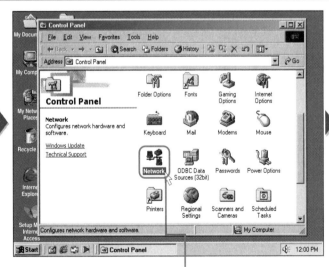

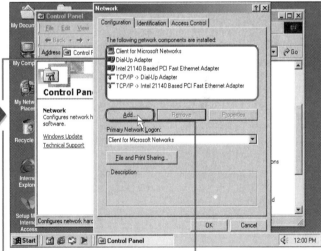

■ All of the items appear in the Control Panel window.

5 Double-click **Network** to change the network settings for your computer.

■ The Network dialog box appears.

■ This area lists the network components installed on your computer. Network protocols display a cable symbol (🍴).

6 Click **Add** to install a new network protocol.

CONTINUED

225

INSTALL A NETWORK PROTOCOL

You must install
the network
protocol required
by the type of
network you want
to connect to.

For example, you
will need to install
the NetBEUI
protocol to connect
to a Windows
network.

INSTALL A NETWORK PROTOCOL (CONTINUED)

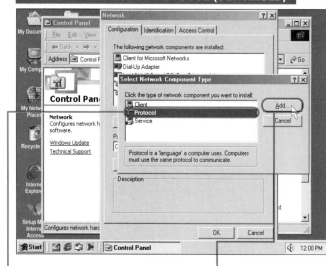

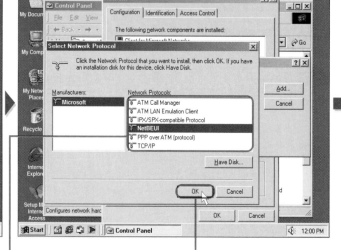

■ The Select Network
Component Type dialog
box appears.

7 Click **Protocol** to add
a new network protocol
to your computer.

8 Click **Add**.

■ The Select Network
Protocol dialog box
appears.

9 Click the network
protocol you want to install.

*Note: For information on the
network protocols you can
install, see the top of page 227.*

10 Click **OK** to confirm
your selection.

What network protocols can I install?

Windows offers many network protocols that you can install. Here are the most common network protocols.

NetBEUI

NetBEUI is a network protocol that allows computers on a Windows network to communicate.

TCP/IP

TCP/IP is a network protocol that allows computers to connect to the Internet. When you first install Windows, TCP/IP is automatically installed on your computer.

IPX/SPX

IPX/SPX is a network protocol that allows computers on a Novell network to communicate.

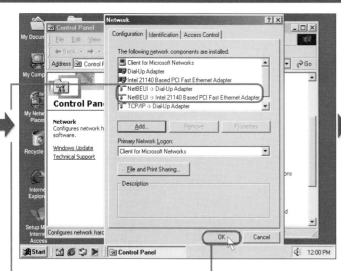

■ Windows adds the network protocol to the list of network components.

Note: If the protocol appears more than once in the list, Windows has set up the protocol to work with several devices, such as a modem and network card.

11 Click **OK** to install the network protocol.

■ The System Settings Change dialog box appears, stating that Windows needs to restart your computer before the new settings will take effect.

12 Click **Yes** to restart your computer.

SHARE INFORMATION

You can specify the information on your computer that you want to share with other people on a network.

Before you can share information, you must turn on sharing. To turn on sharing, see page 220.

Sharing information is useful when people on a network are working together on a project and need to access the same files.

SHARE INFORMATION

1 Click the folder you want to share.

2 Click **File**.

3 Click **Sharing**.

■ The Properties dialog box appears.

4 Click **Shared As:** to share the folder with other people on your network (○ changes to ⊙).

What types of access can I assign to a folder?

You can assign one of three types of access to a folder on your computer.

Read-Only

All individuals on the network can read and copy files but cannot change or delete files.

Full

All individuals on the network can read, copy, change, add and delete files.

Depends on Password

Some individuals on the network have Read-Only access, while others have Full access, depending on which password they enter.

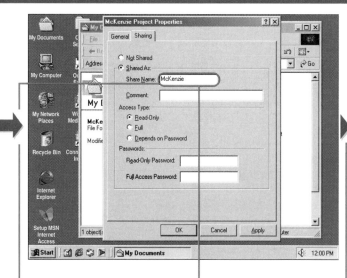

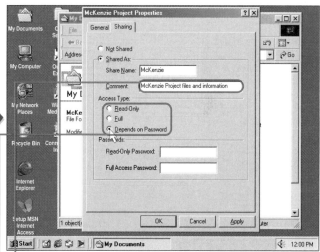

■ This area displays the name of the folder people will see on the network.

5 To assign a new name to the folder, drag the mouse I over the text until the text is highlighted. Then type a new name.

Note: A folder name cannot contain more than 12 characters.

6 To enter a comment about the folder that people can see on the network, click this area and then type a comment.

7 Click the type of access you want to assign to the folder (○ changes to ⊙).

Note: For information on the types of access you can assign to a folder, see the top of this page.

CONTINUED ▶

SHARE INFORMATION

You can assign a password to a shared folder on your computer to prevent unauthorized people from accessing the folder.

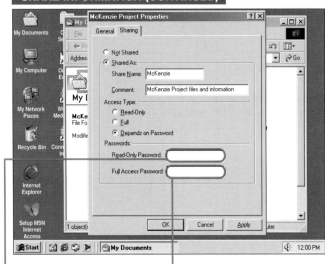

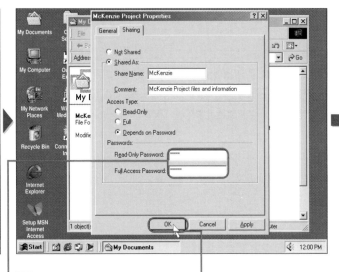

8 If you selected Read-Only in step **7** and want to assign a password, click this area and type a password.

Note: A symbol (ˣ) appears for each character you type to prevent others from seeing the password.

9 If you selected Full in step **7** and want to assign a password, click this area and type a password.

10 If you selected Depends on Password in step **7**, perform steps **8** and **9** to enter both a Read-Only and Full access password.

Note: The passwords for Read-Only and Full access must be different.

11 Click **OK** to confirm your changes.

What password should I use?

You should follow these guidelines when choosing a password.

- ✔ A password can contain up to 8 characters.

- ✔ A password should contain a mixture of letters and numbers.

- ✘ A password should not be a word in the dictionary.

- ✘ A password should not contain your name.

How can I view all of the folders that are shared on the network?

You can use **My Network Places** to see a list of all the folders shared by your computer and other computers on the network. To use My Network Places, see page 236.

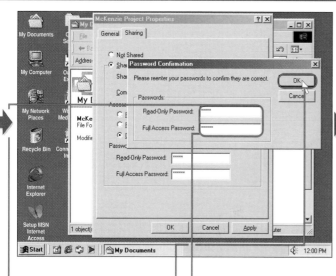

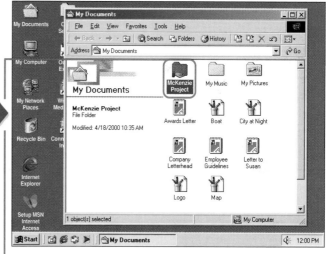

■ The Password Confirmation dialog box appears if you entered a password.

12 Retype the password to confirm the password.

■ If you selected Depends on Password in step **7**, press the Tab key and then retype the Full access password.

13 Click **OK**.

■ Windows displays a hand (👆) under the icon for the shared folder.

■ The folder is now available to other people on the network.

■ To stop sharing a folder, perform steps **1** to **4** on page 228, selecting **Not Shared** in step **4**. Then press the Enter key to confirm your change.

SHARE A PRINTER

You can share your printer with other people on a network. Sharing a printer allows others to use your printer to print documents.

To share your printer, the printer must be directly connected to your computer and sharing must be turned on. To turn on sharing, see page 220.

After you turn on sharing, new printers you install are automatically shared.

SHARE A PRINTER

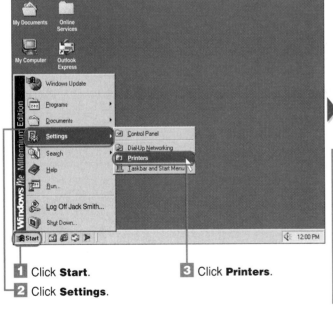

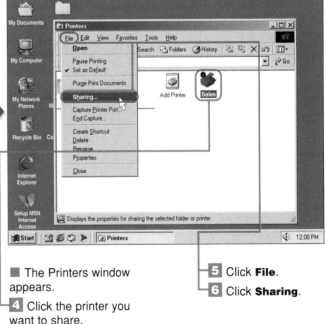

■ Click **Start**.

■ Click **Settings**.

■ Click **Printers**.

■ The Printers window appears.

■ Click the printer you want to share.

■ Click **File**.

■ Click **Sharing**.

What is the main benefit of sharing a printer?

Sharing a printer allows companies to save money since several people on a network can use one printer.

Will sharing a printer affect my computer's performance?

When people on the network send files to your printer, your computer temporarily stores the files before sending them to the printer. As a result, your computer will operate more slowly while other people are using your printer.

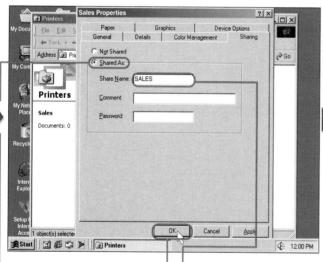

■ The Properties dialog box appears.

7 Click **Shared As:** to share the printer with other people on your network (○ changes to ⊙).

■ This area displays the name of the printer people will see on the network. To change the name, drag the mouse I over the text until the text is highlighted. Then type a new name.

8 Click **OK** to confirm your changes.

■ Windows displays a hand (🖐) under the icon for the shared printer.

■ Your printer is now available to other people on the network.

Note: To use your printer, other people on the network must install the printer on their computers. To install a printer located on the network, see page 186.

■ To stop sharing a printer, repeat steps **1** to **8**, selecting **Not Shared** in step **7**.

CHANGE YOUR DEFAULT PRINTER

If you have access to more than one printer, you can choose which printer you want to automatically print your documents.

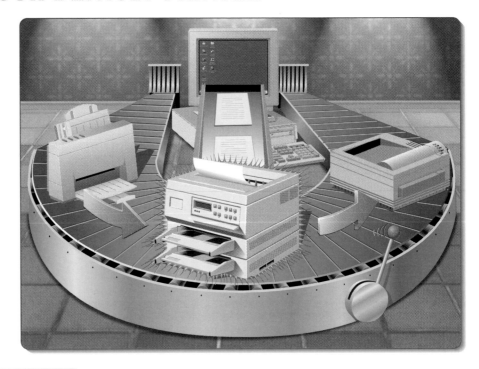

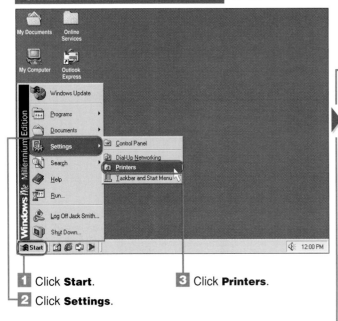

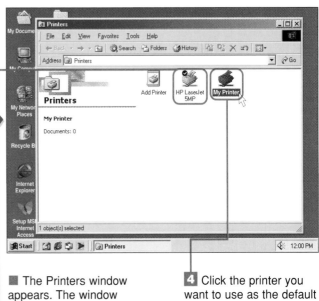

1 Click **Start**.

2 Click **Settings**.

3 Click **Printers**.

■ The Printers window appears. The window displays the printers installed on your computer.

■ The default printer displays a check mark (✔).

4 Click the printer you want to use as the default printer.

234

Which printer should I select as my default printer?

When selecting a default printer, you should choose the printer you use most often. The printer you select should also be close to your desk and offer the capabilities you need.

Can I use a printer that is not my default printer?

You may occasionally want to use another printer to print a document, such as when your default printer is not working properly. When you print a document, most programs will display a dialog box that allows you to select the printer you want to use.

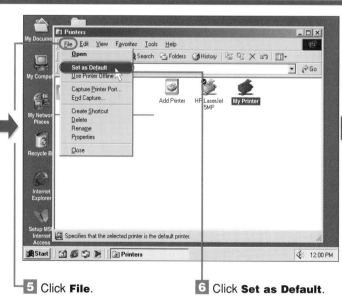

5 Click **File**.

6 Click **Set as Default**.

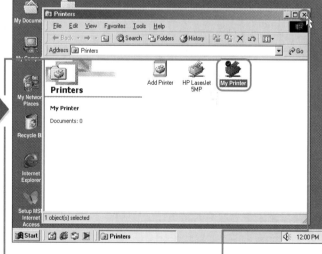

■ The new default printer displays a check mark (✓).

■ Your documents will now automatically print to the new default printer.

7 Click ✕ to close the Printers window.

BROWSE THROUGH A NETWORK

You can easily browse through the information available on your network.

BROWSE THROUGH A NETWORK

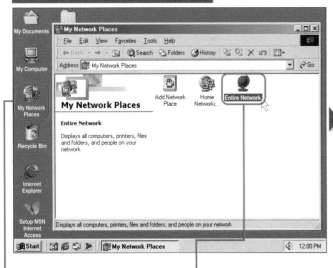

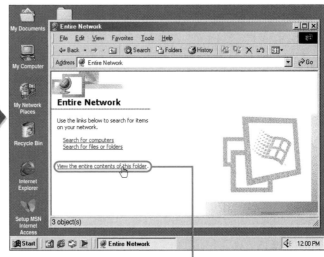

1 Double-click **My Network Places** to browse through the information on your network.

■ The My Network Places window appears.

2 Double-click **Entire Network** to view all the workgroups on your network.

Note: For more information on workgroups, see the top of page 237.

■ The workgroups on your network appear.

3 If the workgroups on your network do not appear, click **View the entire contents of this folder** to display the workgroups.

What do the icons in the My Network Places window represent?

Each item in the My Network Places window displays an icon to help you distinguish between the different types of items.

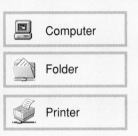 Workgroup

A network consists of one or more groups of computers, called workgroups. The computers in a workgroup frequently share information.

Computer

Folder

Printer

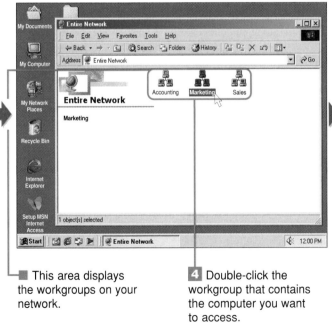

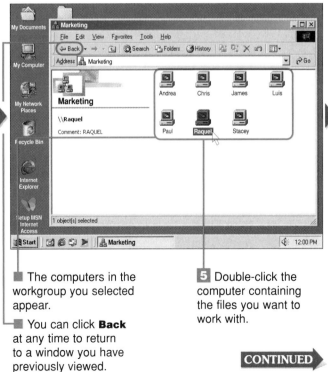

▆ This area displays the workgroups on your network.

4 Double-click the workgroup that contains the computer you want to access.

▆ The computers in the workgroup you selected appear.

▆ You can click **Back** at any time to return to a window you have previously viewed.

5 Double-click the computer containing the files you want to work with.

CONTINUED

BROWSE THROUGH A NETWORK

When accessing a folder on your network, Windows may ask you to enter a password.

If you do not know what password to type, ask your network administrator or the person who owns the folder.

BROWSE THROUGH A NETWORK (CONTINUED)

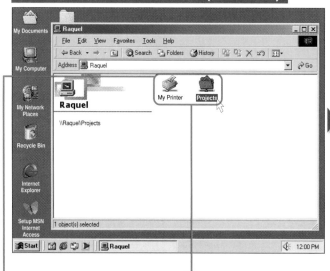

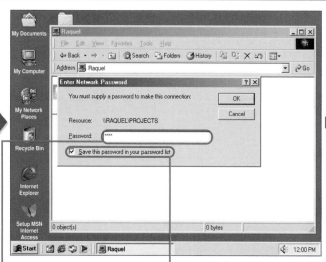

■ The folders and printers shared by the computer appear.

6 Double-click the folder containing the files you want to work with.

■ The Enter Network Password dialog box appears if you must type a password to access the folder.

7 Type the password and then press the **Enter** key.

Note: A symbol (ˣ) appears for each character you type to prevent others from seeing the password.

■ This option saves the password so you do not have to retype the password the next time you access the folder.

Why can I no longer access a folder on my network?

If the computer that stores the folder is turned off or if the owner of the computer decides to stop sharing the folder, you will no longer be able to access the folder.

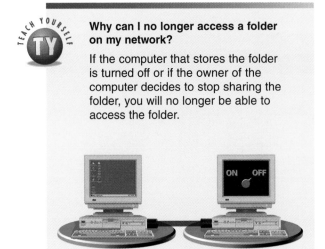

What is the difference between My Computer and My Network Places?

My Computer

Allows you to browse through the contents of your own computer.

My Network Places

Allows you to browse through the contents of other computers on your network.

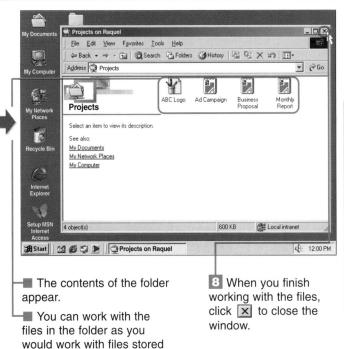

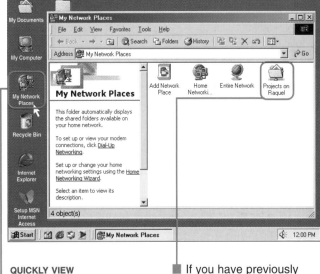

■ The contents of the folder appear.

■ You can work with the files in the folder as you would work with files stored on your own computer.

8 When you finish working with the files, click ✕ to close the window.

QUICKLY VIEW CONTENTS OF A FOLDER

1 Double-click **My Network Places**.

■ If you have previously worked with files in a shared folder on your network, the shared folder appears in the window. You can double-click the folder to quickly view the contents of the folder.

SEARCH FOR A COMPUTER ON A NETWORK

You can quickly locate a computer on your network. Searching for a computer is useful if your network contains many computers.

SEARCH FOR A COMPUTER ON A NETWORK

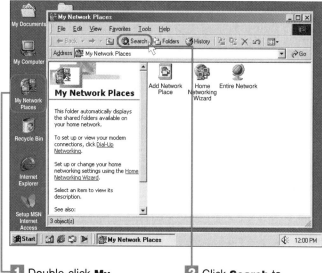

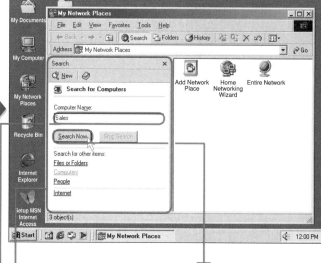

1 Double-click **My Network Places**.

■ The My Network Places window appears.

2 Click **Search** to search for a computer on your network.

■ An area appears that allows you to search for a computer on your network.

3 Click this area and then type the name of the computer you want to find.

4 Click **Search Now** to start the search.

Can I search for a computer on my network if I know only part of the computer's name?

You can use an asterisk (*) to help you find a computer on your network when you know only part of the computer's name. The asterisk (*) can represent one or more characters. For example, type **Jon*** to find computers with names that begin with Jon, such as **Jon**athon.

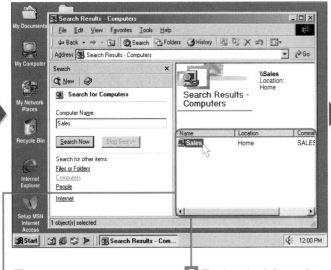

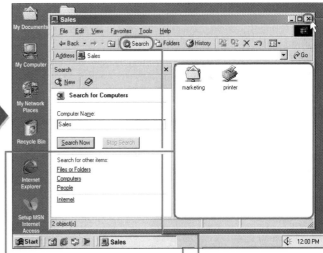

■ This area displays the name of each computer that matches the name you specified.

5 To view the information and equipment shared by a computer, double-click the name of the computer.

■ The items shared by the computer appears.

■ You can work with the information shared by the computer as you would work with information stored on your own computer.

Note: You may be asked to type a password to access some shared items.

■ To hide the search area, click **Search**.

6 When you finish working with information on your network, click ✕ to close the window.

SET UP A HOME NETWORK

If you have more than one computer at home, you can set up a network so you can exchange information between the computers.

A network allows you to work with files stored on other computers on the network. A network also allows several computers to share one printer.

Before setting up your home network, you need to install and set up your network hardware. Network hardware allows the computers on your network to communicate.

Internet Connection

One computer on the network will need a device, such as a modem, to connect to the Internet. The computer can share its Internet connection with other computers on the network. Computers on a network that share an Internet connection can access the Internet at the same time.

Network Interface Card

A Network Interface Card (NIC) connects each computer to the network and controls the flow of information between the network and the computers. NICs are installed inside a computer and are also called network adapters.

Cables

Cables physically connect each computer to the network.

Software

One computer on the network must use Windows Me. Other computers on the network must use Windows 95, Windows 98 or Windows Me.

Hub

A network may require a hub, which provides a central location where the cables on the network meet.

Windows provides the Home Networking Wizard that will take you step by step through the process of setting up a computer on your home network.

You must run the Home Networking Wizard on each computer you want to set up on your home network.

SET UP A HOME NETWORK

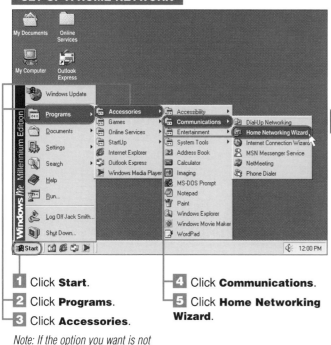

1 Click **Start**.

2 Click **Programs**.

3 Click **Accessories**.

Note: If the option you want is not displayed on a menu, position the mouse over the bottom of the menu to display all the options.

4 Click **Communications**.

5 Click **Home Networking Wizard**.

■ The Home Networking Wizard appears.

■ This area displays information about the wizard as well as a reminder that your network hardware should be installed and set up correctly before you use the wizard.

Note: For information on the network hardware you need, see page 242.

6 Click **Next** to continue.

CONTINUED

SET UP A HOME NETWORK

You can set up a computer on your home network to share its connection to the Internet with other computers on the network.

Computers on a network can use one Internet connection to access the Internet at the same time.

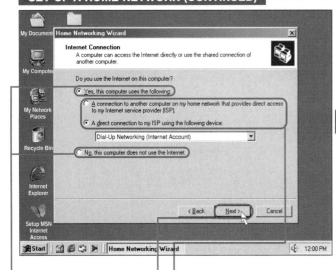

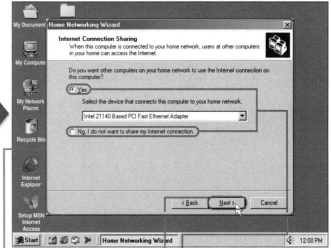

7 Click **Yes** or **No** to specify if you want to connect to the Internet from this computer (○ changes to ⊙).

8 If you selected **Yes** in step **7**, click an option to specify how you want to connect to the Internet (○ changes to ⊙). You can connect to the Internet through a shared connection on another computer or directly through this computer.

9 Click **Next** to continue.

■ This screen appears if you chose to connect to the Internet directly through this computer.

Note: If this screen does not appear, skip to step 16 on page 246.

10 Click **Yes** or **No** to specify if you want to share your connection to the Internet with other computers on your network (○ changes to ⊙).

11 Click **Next** to continue.

What should I consider when sharing an Internet connection on my network?

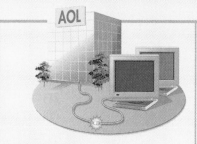

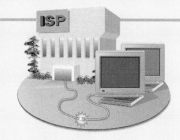

AOL Members

If you use America Online (AOL), you may not be able to share an Internet connection. You can contact AOL for more information.

Internet Service Providers

An Internet Service Provider (ISP) is a company that gives you access to the Internet. Your ISP may not allow more than one computer on your network to connect to the Internet through a single Internet connection. You can contact your ISP for more information.

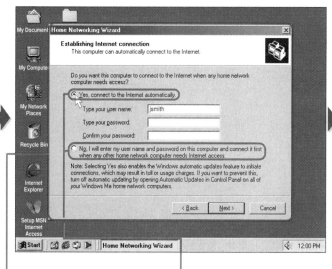

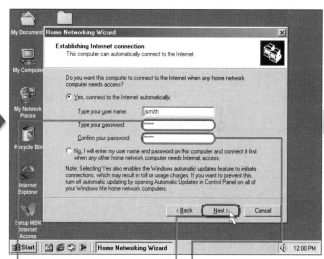

■ This screen may appear if you chose to share your Internet connection.

*Note: If this screen does not appear, skip to step **16** on page 246.*

12 Click **Yes** or **No** to specify if you want your computer to automatically connect to the Internet when another computer wants to access the Internet (○ changes to ⊙).

*Note: If you specify **No** in step **12**, you will need to enter your password on your computer before another computer can access the Internet.*

13 If you selected **Yes** in step **12**, click this area and type your password.

Note: A symbol (ˣ) appears for each character you type to prevent other people from seeing your password.

14 Click this area and retype your password to confirm the password.

15 Click **Next** to continue.

CONTINUED ▶

When setting up a computer on your home network, you need to provide a computer name and workgroup name for the computer.

A computer name identifies a computer on your network. Each computer on a network must have a different name.

A workgroup name identifies a group of computers on your network. Each computer in a workgroup must have the same workgroup name.

SET UP A HOME NETWORK (CONTINUED)

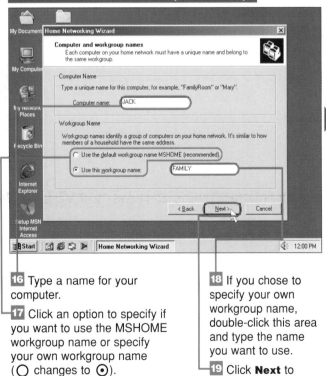

16 Type a name for your computer.

17 Click an option to specify if you want to use the MSHOME workgroup name or specify your own workgroup name (○ changes to ⊙).

18 If you chose to specify your own workgroup name, double-click this area and type the name you want to use.

19 Click **Next** to continue.

20 This option allows you to share the My Documents folder on your computer with other people on your network. Click this option if you want to share the folder (□ changes to ☑).

21 If you chose to share the My Documents folder, click **Password** to assign a password that will prevent unauthorized people from accessing the folder.

**What folders can I share with
other computers on my home
network?**

The Home Networking Wizard
allows you to share the My
Documents folder on your
computer.

The My Documents folder is
located on your desktop. This
folder provides a convenient
place to store your files. Many
programs automatically store
files you save in the My
Documents folder.

After you complete
the Home Networking
Wizard, you can
share other folders
on your computer.
To share other folders
on your computer,
see page 228.

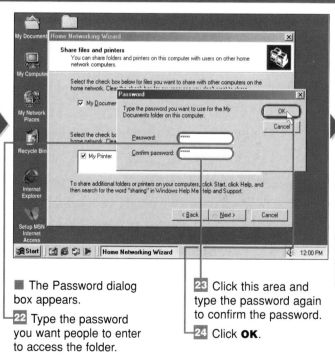

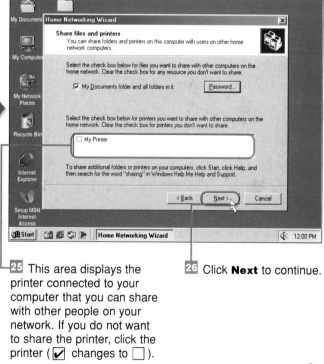

■ The Password dialog
box appears.

22 Type the password
you want people to enter
to access the folder.

23 Click this area and
type the password again
to confirm the password.

24 Click **OK**.

25 This area displays the
printer connected to your
computer that you can share
with other people on your
network. If you do not want
to share the printer, click the
printer (☑ changes to ☐).

26 Click **Next** to continue.

CONTINUED ▶

SET UP A HOME NETWORK

You can create a Home
Networking Setup disk
that will allow you to
set up other computers
that use Windows 95
or Windows 98 on your
home network.

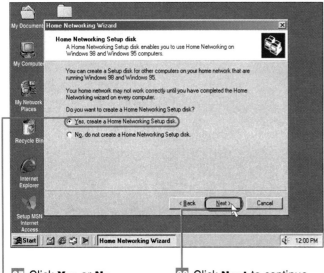

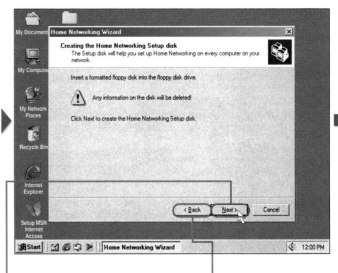

27 Click **Yes** or **No**
to specify if you want
to create a Home
Networking Setup disk
(○ changes to ⊙).

28 Click **Next** to continue.

*Note: If you chose **No** in step 27,
skip to step 32.*

29 Insert a formatted floppy
disk into your floppy drive.
Windows will delete any
information on the floppy disk.

30 Click **Next** to create the
Home Networking Setup disk.

■ You can click **Back**
at any time to return to
a previous screen and
change your selections.

TEACH YOURSELF: How do I set up a Windows 95 or Windows 98 computer on my home network?

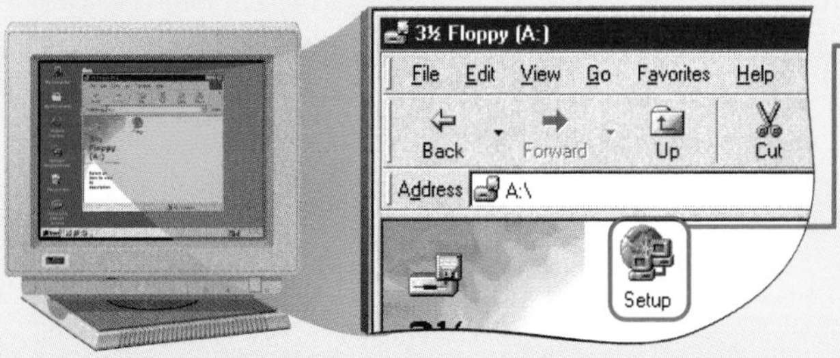

1 After creating a Home Networking Setup disk on a Windows Me computer as shown on page 248, insert the floppy disk into your Windows 95 or Windows 98 computer.

2 Display the contents of the floppy disk. To display the contents of a floppy disk, see page 48.

3 Double-click **Setup** to start the Home Networking Wizard.

4 Follow the instructions on your screen to set up the computer on your home network.

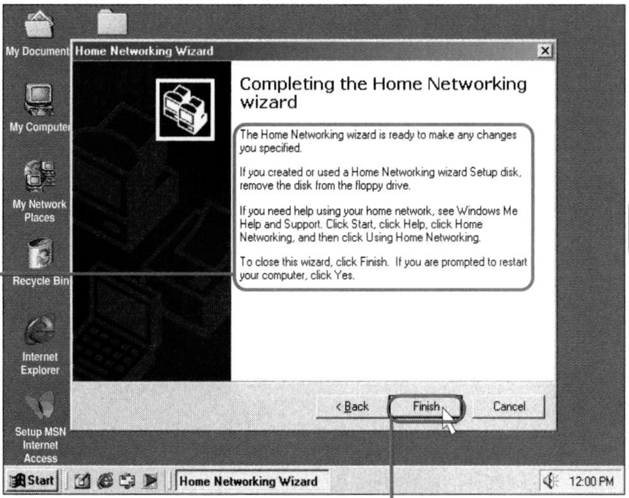

■ This message appears when you have completed the Home Networking Wizard.

31 If you created a Home Networking Setup disk, remove the floppy disk from your floppy drive.

32 Click **Finish** to complete the setup.

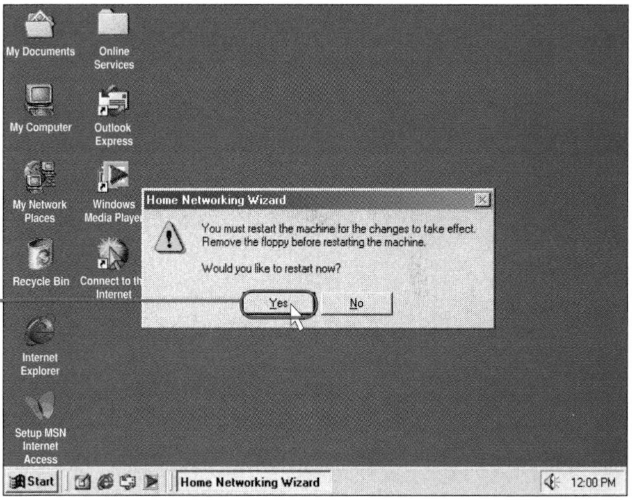

■ A message appears, stating that you must restart your computer before the changes will take effect.

33 Click **Yes** to restart your computer.

■ After your computer restarts, a dialog box will appear to confirm that home networking is set up on the computer. Click **OK** to close the dialog box.

■ You must now run the Home Networking Wizard on each computer you want to set up on your home network.

CHAPTER 11

Browse the Web

This chapter will explain how the World Wide Web works and how you can use it to transfer information to your computer from Web sites around the world.

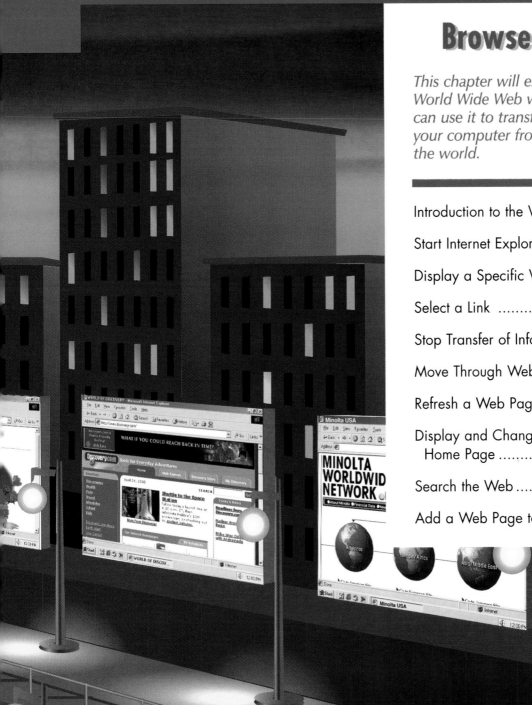

INTRODUCTION TO THE WEB

The World Wide Web is part of the Internet, which is the largest computer system in the world. The Web consists of a huge collection of documents stored on millions of computers.

WEB PAGE

A Web page is a document on the Web. Web pages can include text, pictures, sound and video. You can find Web pages on every subject imaginable. Web pages can offer information such as newspaper and magazine articles, movie clips, recipes, Shakespearean plays, airline schedules and more.

WEB SERVER

A Web server is a computer that stores Web pages and makes the pages available on the Web for other people to view.

WEB SITE

A Web site is a collection of Web pages created and maintained by a college, university, government agency, company or individual.

Each Web site can only allow a certain number of people to connect at once. If you are unable to connect to a Web site, try connecting at a later time.

URL

Each Web page has a unique address, called a Uniform Resource Locator (URL). You can display any Web page if you know its URL. Most Web page URLs start with http (HyperText Transfer Protocol).

LINKS

Web pages usually contain links, which are highlighted text or images on a Web page that connect to other pages on the Web. You can select a link to display a Web page located on the same computer or on a computer across the city, country or world.

Links allow you to easily navigate through a vast amount of information by jumping from one Web page to another. This is known as "browsing the Web."

CONNECTING TO THE INTERNET

Most people use an Internet Service Provider (ISP) to connect to the Internet. Once you pay your ISP to connect to the Internet, you can view and exchange information on the Internet free of charge.

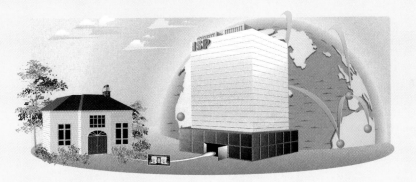

Most individuals use a modem to connect to the Internet, although cable modems, Integrated Services Digital Network (ISDN) lines and Digital Subscriber Lines (DSL) are becoming more popular. Most schools and businesses connect to the Internet through a network connection.

START INTERNET EXPLORER

You can start
Internet Explorer
to browse through
the information
on the Web.

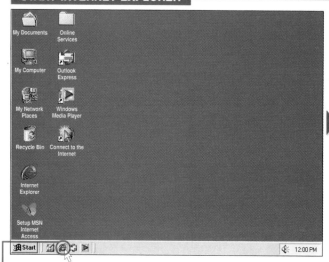

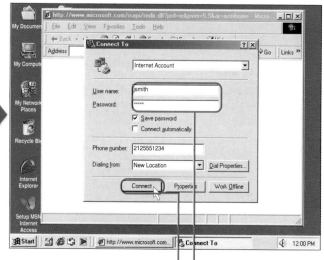

1 Click 🌐 to start
Internet Explorer.

*Note: If the Internet Connection
Wizard appears, see the top of
page 255.*

■ The Microsoft Internet
Explorer window appears.

■ If you are not currently
connected to the Internet,
the Connect To dialog box
also appears.

■ This area displays your
user name and password.

*Note: A symbol (×) appears for
each character in your password
to prevent others from viewing
the password.*

2 Click **Connect** to
connect to the Internet.

Why does the Internet Connection Wizard appear when I try to start Internet Explorer?

The Internet Connection Wizard appears the first time you start Internet Explorer to help you get connected to the Internet. You can use the wizard to set up a new or existing account on the Internet. To set up an existing account, you will need to ask your Internet Service Provider (ISP) for the information you need to enter.

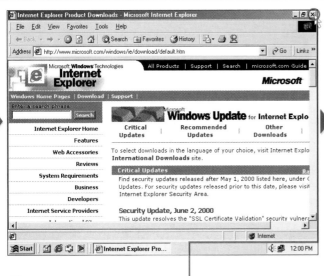

■ Once you are connected to the Internet, the Microsoft Internet Explorer window displays your home page.

Note: To maximize the Microsoft Internet Explorer window to fill your screen, see page 14.

EXIT INTERNET EXPLORER

1 When you finish browsing through information on the Web, click ⌧ to close the Microsoft Internet Explorer window.

■ A dialog box appears, asking if you want to disconnect from the Internet.

2 Click **Disconnect Now**.

■ This icon (🖳) appears on the taskbar when you are connected to the Internet. The icon disappears when you disconnect from the Internet.

DISPLAY A SPECIFIC WEB PAGE

You can display a page on the Web that you have heard or read about.

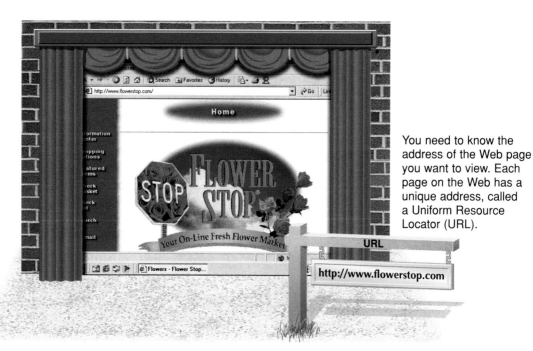

You need to know the address of the Web page you want to view. Each page on the Web has a unique address, called a Uniform Resource Locator (URL).

URL

http://www.flowerstop.com

DISPLAY A SPECIFIC WEB PAGE

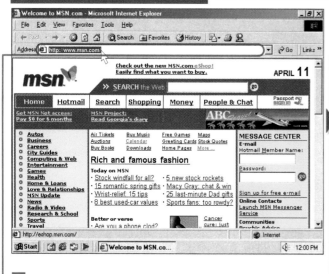

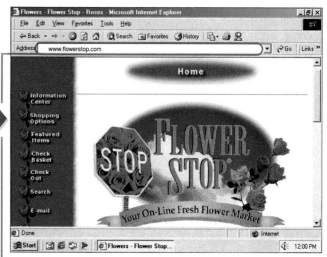

1 Click this area to highlight the current Web page address.

2 Type the address of the Web page you want to display and then press the **Enter** key.

*Note: You do not need to type **http://** when typing a Web page address.*

■ The Web page appears on your screen.

What are some popular Web pages that I can display?

Blue Mountain Arts	www.bluemountain.com
CBS SportsLine	www.sportsline.com
CNN.com	www.cnn.com
eBay	www.ebay.com
maranGraphics	www.maran.com
MSNBC	www.msnbc.com
MTV.com	www.mtv.com
NASA	www.nasa.gov
Sony	www.sony.com
TIME.com	www.time.com

REDISPLAY A WEB PAGE

Internet Explorer remembers the addresses of Web pages you recently visited. You can select one of these addresses to quickly redisplay a Web page.

1 When you begin typing the address of a Web page you recently visited, a list of matching addresses appears.

2 Click the address of the Web page you want to display.

■ The Web page appears on your screen.

■ You can also click ▾ to display a list of addresses you recently visited.

SELECT A LINK

A link connects text or an image on one Web page to another Web page. When you select the text or image, the linked Web page appears.

SELECT A LINK

 **1** Position the mouse ⌖ over a highlighted word or image of interest. The mouse ⌖ changes to a hand ⌐ when over a link.

2 Click the word or image to display the linked Web page.

■ The linked Web page appears.

■ This area displays the name of the Web page.

■ This icon is animated as the Web page transfers to your computer.

■ This area displays the address of the Web page.

STOP TRANSFER OF INFORMATION

rowse the Web **11**

If a Web page is
taking a long time
to appear on your
screen, you can
stop the transfer
of the page and
try displaying the
page later.

STOP TRANSFER OF INFORMATION

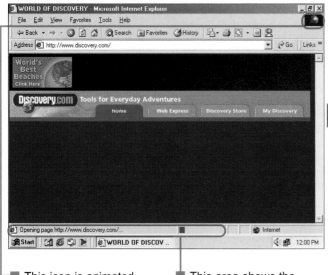

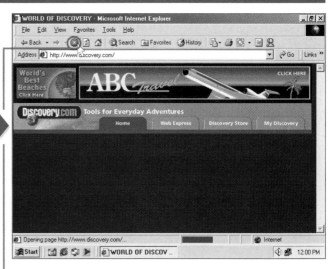

■ This icon is animated when information is transferring to your computer.

■ This area shows the progress of the transfer.

1 Click to stop the transfer of information.

■ You may also want to stop the transfer of information if you realize a Web page contains information that does not interest you.

259

MOVE THROUGH WEB PAGES

You can easily move back and forth through the Web pages you have viewed since you last started Internet Explorer.

MOVE THROUGH WEB PAGES

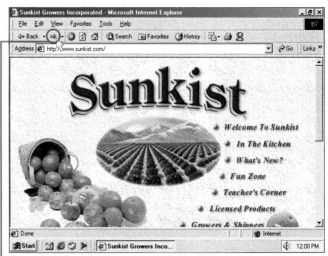

MOVE BACK

1 Click **Back** to return to the last Web page you viewed.

*Note: The **Back** button is only available if you have viewed other Web pages since you last started Internet Explorer.*

MOVE FORWARD

1 Click ⇨ to move forward through the Web pages you have viewed.

*Note: The ⇨ button is only available after you use the **Back** button to return to a Web page.*

You can refresh a Web page to update the information displayed on your screen. Internet Explorer will transfer a fresh copy of the Web page to your computer.

Refreshing a Web page is useful for updating information such as the current news, sports scores and stock market data.

REFRESH A WEB PAGE

1 Click 🗘 to transfer a fresh copy of the displayed Web page to your computer.

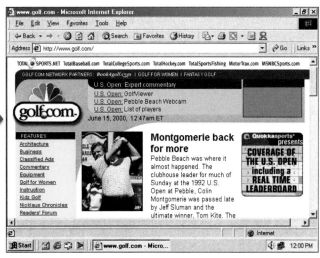

■ A fresh copy of the Web page appears on your screen.

DISPLAY AND CHANGE YOUR HOME PAGE

You can specify which Web page you want to appear each time you start Internet Explorer. This page is called your home page.

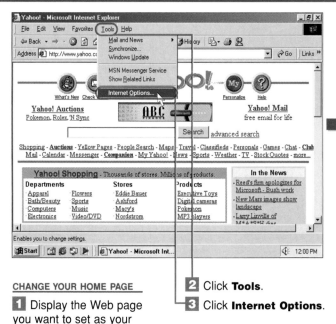

DISPLAY YOUR HOME PAGE

1 Click 🏠 to display your home page.

■ Your home page appears.

Note: Your home page may be different than the home page shown above.

CHANGE YOUR HOME PAGE

1 Display the Web page you want to set as your home page.

Note: To display a Web page, see page 256.

2 Click **Tools**.

3 Click **Internet Options**.

Which Web page should I set as my home page?

You can set any page on the Web as your home page. Your home page can be a Web page you frequently visit or a Web page that provides a good starting point for exploring the Web.

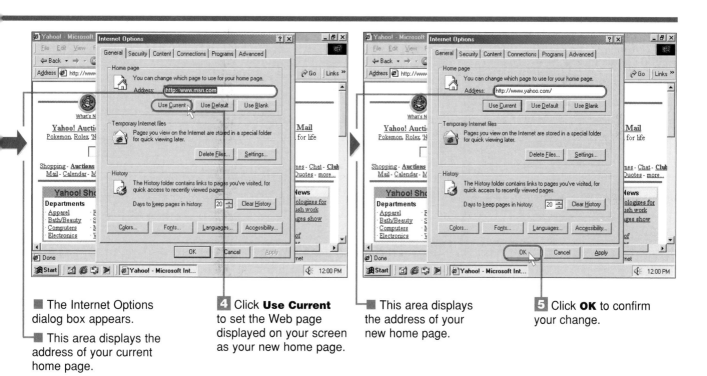

■ The Internet Options dialog box appears.

■ This area displays the address of your current home page.

4 Click **Use Current** to set the Web page displayed on your screen as your new home page.

■ This area displays the address of your new home page.

5 Click **OK** to confirm your change.

SEARCH THE WEB

You can search for
Web pages that
discuss topics of
interest to you.

SEARCH THE WEB

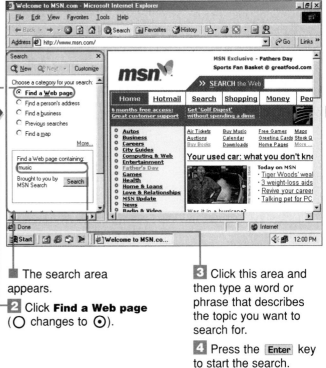

1 Click **Search** to
search for Web pages
of interest.

■ The search area
appears.

2 Click **Find a Web page**
(○ changes to ⊙).

3 Click this area and
then type a word or
phrase that describes
the topic you want to
search for.

4 Press the Enter key
to start the search.

Is there another way to search for information on the Web?

You can use a search tool on the Web to search for Web pages that discuss topics of interest to you. Many search tools allow you to browse through categories, such as entertainment, news and sports, to find interesting Web pages. Here are some popular search tools that you can use.

AltaVista
www.altavista.com

Lycos
www.lycos.com

Yahoo!
www.yahoo.com

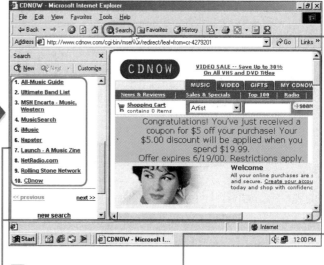

■ A list of matching Web pages appears. You can use the scroll bar to view the entire list.

5 To display a description of a Web page, position the mouse ⌖ over the Web page (⌖ changes to ⟨ᑦᒻᕁ⟩).

■ A yellow box appears, displaying a description of the Web page.

6 Click the Web page you want to display.

■ The Web page you selected appears in this area.

Note: To display another Web page, repeat step 6.

7 When you have finished displaying Web pages of interest, you can click **Search** to hide the search area.

ADD A WEB PAGE TO FAVORITES

You can use the Favorites feature to create a list of Web pages you frequently visit. You can quickly display any Web page in the list.

ADD A WEB PAGE TO FAVORITES

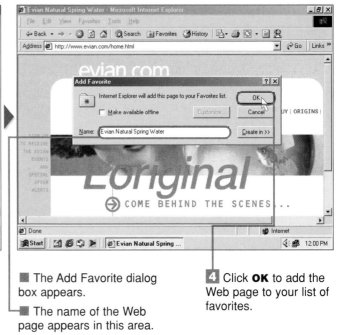

1 Display the Web page you want to add to your list of favorite Web pages.

Note: To display a Web page, see page 256.

2 Click **Favorites**.

3 Click **Add to Favorites**.

■ The Add Favorite dialog box appears.

■ The name of the Web page appears in this area.

4 Click **OK** to add the Web page to your list of favorites.

**What are the benefits of adding a
Web page to my list of favorites?**

Web page addresses can be long and
complex. Selecting Web pages from
your list of favorites saves you from
having to remember and constantly
retype the same addresses over and
over again.

**Does Internet Explorer automatically
add Web pages to my list of favorites?**

Yes. In your list of favorites, Internet
Explorer provides the Links and Media
folders that contain the names of popular
Web pages you may find useful. These
folders allow you to quickly access Web
pages such as Best of the Web, CBS
and Hollywood Online.

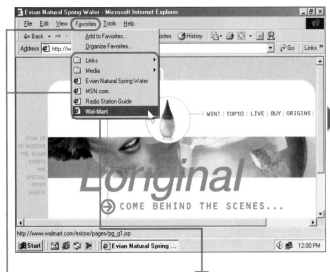

VIEW A FAVORITE WEB PAGE

1 Click **Favorites**.

■ A list of your favorite
Web pages appears.

*Note: If the entire list does not
appear, position the mouse
over the bottom of the menu
to display the entire list.*

2 Click the favorite Web
page you want to view.

*Note: To display the favorite
Web pages in a folder, click
the folder ( ).*

■ The favorite Web page
you selected appears.

■ You can repeat steps **1**
and **2** to view another
favorite Web page.

CHAPTER 12

Exchange Electronic Mail

Exchange e-mail messages with friends, family members and colleagues from around the world. This chapter will show you how to read, send and print e-mail messages.

You can start Outlook Express to exchange e-mail messages with people around the world.

E-mail provides a fast, economical and convenient way to exchange messages with family, friends and colleagues.

START OUTLOOK EXPRESS

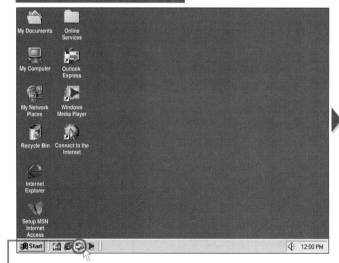

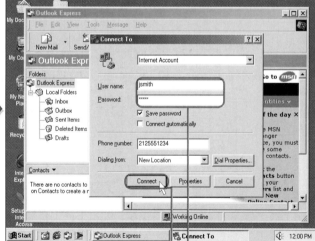

1 Click 📧 to start Outlook Express.

Note: If the Internet Connection Wizard appears, see the top of page 255.

■ The Outlook Express window appears.

■ If you are not currently connected to the Internet, the Connect To dialog box also appears.

■ This area displays your user name and password.

Note: A symbol (ˣ) appears for each character in your password to prevent others from viewing the password.

2 Click **Connect** to connect to the Internet.

What are the parts of an e-mail address?

You can send a message to anyone around the world if you know the person's e-mail address. An e-mail address defines the location of an individual's mailbox on the Internet.

An e-mail address consists of two parts separated by the @ (at) symbol. An e-mail address cannot contain spaces.

The **user name** is the name of the person's account and can be a real name or a nickname.

The **domain name** is the location of the person's account on the Internet. Periods (.) separate the various parts of the domain name.

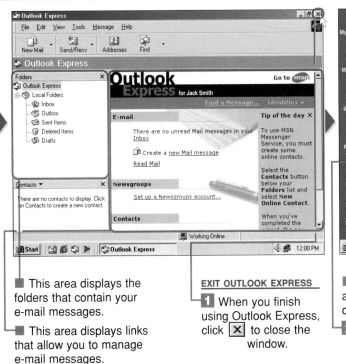

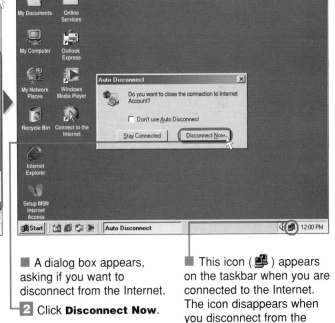

■ This area displays the folders that contain your e-mail messages.

■ This area displays links that allow you to manage e-mail messages.

Note: To maximize the Outlook Express window to fill your screen, see page 14.

EXIT OUTLOOK EXPRESS

1 When you finish using Outlook Express, click ☒ to close the window.

■ A dialog box appears, asking if you want to disconnect from the Internet.

2 Click **Disconnect Now**.

■ This icon (🖳) appears on the taskbar when you are connected to the Internet. The icon disappears when you disconnect from the Internet.

READ MESSAGES

You can easily open your messages to read their contents.

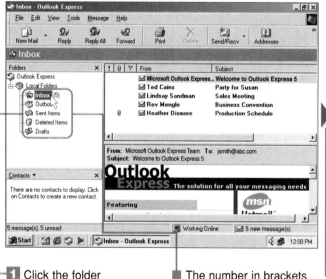

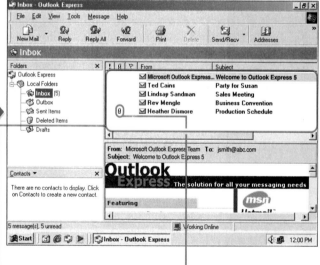

1 Click the folder containing the messages you want to read. The folder is highlighted.

■ The number in brackets beside the folder indicates how many unread messages the folder contains. The number disappears when you have read all the messages in the folder.

■ This area displays the messages in the folder you selected. Messages you have not read display a closed envelope (✉) and appear in **bold** type.

■ A paper clip icon (📎) appears beside a message with an attached file.

Note: To open an attached file, see page 284.

What folders does Outlook Express use to store my messages?

Inbox	**Outbox**	**Sent Items**	**Deleted Items**	**Drafts**
Stores messages sent to you.	Temporarily stores messages that have not yet been sent.	Stores copies of messages you have sent.	Stores messages you have deleted.	Stores messages you have not yet completed.

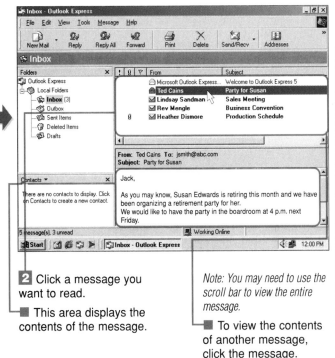

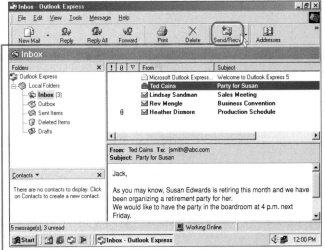

2 Click a message you want to read.

■ This area displays the contents of the message.

Note: You may need to use the scroll bar to view the entire message.

■ To view the contents of another message, click the message.

CHECK FOR NEW MESSAGES

Outlook Express automatically checks for new messages every 30 minutes.

1 To immediately check for new messages, click **Send/Recv**.

Note: A dialog box may appear, asking for your password. Type the password for your e-mail account and then press the Enter *key.*

SEND A MESSAGE

You can send a
message to express
an idea or request
information.

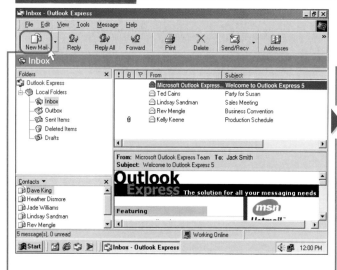

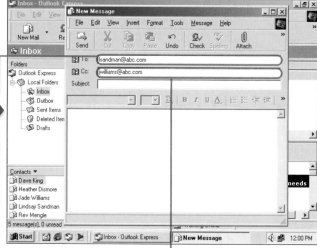

1 Click **New Mail** to
send a new message.

■ The New Message
window appears.

2 Type the e-mail
address of the person
you want to receive
the message.

3 To send a copy of the
message to a person who is
not directly involved but would
be interested in the message,
click this area and then type
the e-mail address.

*Note: To send the message to more
than one person, separate each
e-mail address with a semicolon (;).*

How can I express emotions in my e-mail messages?

You can use special characters, called smileys, to express emotions in e-mail messages. These characters resemble human faces if you turn them sideways.

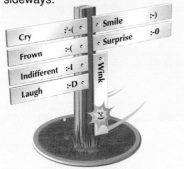

Cry :'-(
Smile :-)
Frown :-(
Surprise :-0
Indifferent :-I
Wink
Laugh :-D
:-)

What should I consider when sending a message?

A MESSAGE WRITTEN IN CAPITAL LETTERS IS ANNOYING AND DIFFICULT TO READ. THIS IS CALLED SHOUTING. Always use upper and lower case letters when typing e-mail messages.

HOW ARE YOU?

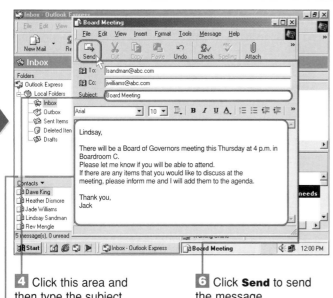

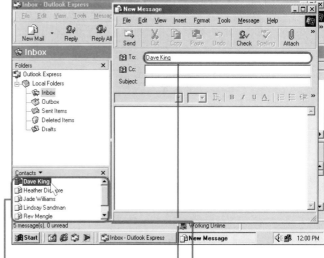

4 Click this area and then type the subject of the message.

5 Click this area and then type the message.

6 Click **Send** to send the message.

■ Outlook Express stores a copy of each message you send in the Sent Items folder.

QUICKLY ADDRESS A MESSAGE

■ The Contacts list displays the name of each person in your address book.

Note: For information on the address book, see page 286.

1 To quickly send a message to a person in the Contacts list, double-click the name of the person.

■ The New Message window appears.

■ Outlook Express addresses the message for you.

SAVE A DRAFT OF A MESSAGE

You can save a draft of a message that you want to send at a later time. Saving a draft of a message allows you to later review and make changes to the message before sending the message.

SAVE A DRAFT OF A MESSAGE

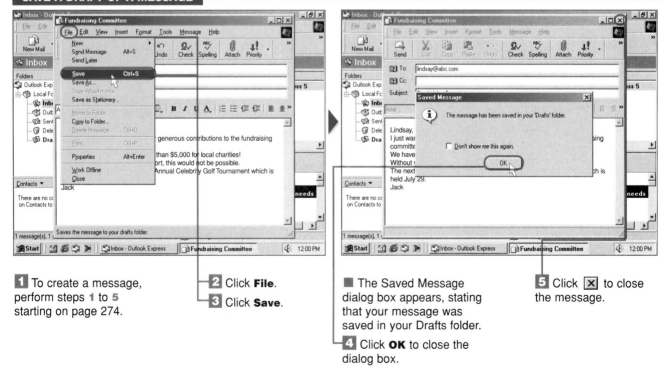

1 To create a message, perform steps **1** to **5** starting on page 274.

2 Click **File**.

3 Click **Save**.

■ The Saved Message dialog box appears, stating that your message was saved in your Drafts folder.

4 Click **OK** to close the dialog box.

5 Click ☒ to close the message.

I no longer want to send a message I saved as a draft. What can I do?

If you no longer want to send a message you saved as a draft, you can delete the message from the Drafts folder as you would delete any message. To delete a message, see page 285.

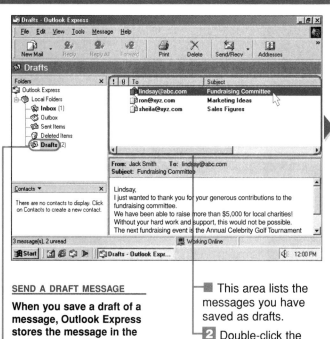

SEND A DRAFT MESSAGE

When you save a draft of a message, Outlook Express stores the message in the Drafts folder until you are ready to send the message.

1 Click the **Drafts** folder.

■ This area lists the messages you have saved as drafts.

2 Double-click the message you want to send.

■ A window appears, displaying the contents of the message. You can review and make changes to the message.

3 To send the message, click **Send**.

REPLY TO A MESSAGE

You can reply to a message to answer a question or comment on the message.

REPLY TO A MESSAGE

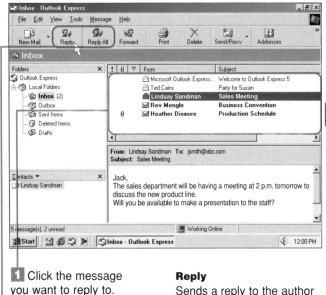

1 Click the message you want to reply to.

2 Click the reply option you want to use.

Reply

Sends a reply to the author only.

Reply All

Sends a reply to the author and everyone who received the original message.

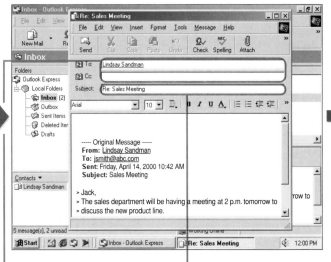

■ A window appears for you to compose the message.

■ Outlook Express fills in the e-mail address(es) for you.

■ Outlook Express also fills in the subject, starting the subject with **Re:**.

How can I save time when typing a message?

Abbreviations for words and phrases are commonly used to save time when typing messages.

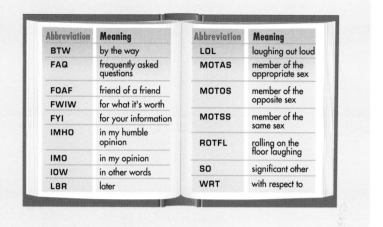

Abbreviation	Meaning
BTW	by the way
FAQ	frequently asked questions
FOAF	friend of a friend
FWIW	for what it's worth
FYI	for your information
IMHO	in my humble opinion
IMO	in my opinion
IOW	in other words
L8R	later

Abbreviation	Meaning
LOL	laughing out loud
MOTAS	member of the appropriate sex
MOTOS	member of the opposite sex
MOTSS	member of the same sex
ROTFL	rolling on the floor laughing
SO	significant other
WRT	with respect to

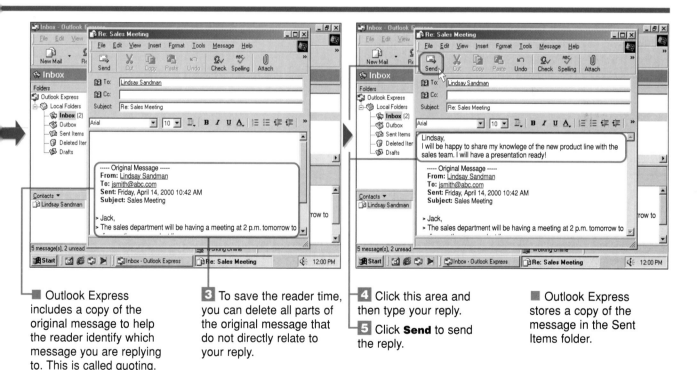

■ Outlook Express includes a copy of the original message to help the reader identify which message you are replying to. This is called quoting.

3 To save the reader time, you can delete all parts of the original message that do not directly relate to your reply.

4 Click this area and then type your reply.

5 Click **Send** to send the reply.

■ Outlook Express stores a copy of the message in the Sent Items folder.

FORWARD A MESSAGE

After reading a message, you can add comments and then forward the message to a friend or colleague.

FORWARD A MESSAGE

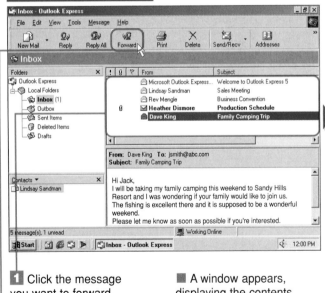

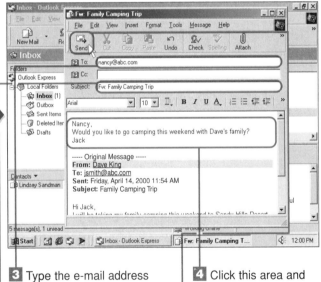

1 Click the message you want to forward.

2 Click **Forward**.

■ A window appears, displaying the contents of the message you are forwarding.

3 Type the e-mail address of the person you want to receive the message.

Note: To select a name from the address book, see page 290.

■ Outlook Express fills in the subject for you, starting the subject with **Fw:**.

4 Click this area and then type any comments about the message you are forwarding.

5 Click Send to forward the message.

You can produce
a paper copy of
a message you
received.

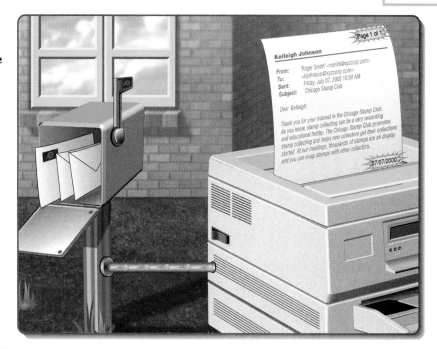

Outlook Express
prints the page
number and total
number of pages at
the top of each page.
The current date
prints at the bottom
of each page.

PRINT A MESSAGE

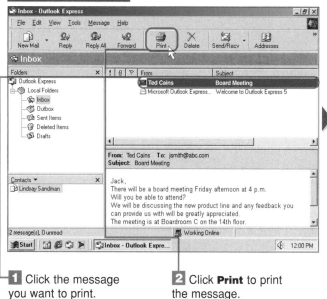

1 Click the message
you want to print.

2 Click **Print** to print
the message.

■ The Print dialog box
appears.

3 Click **OK** to print
the entire message.

ATTACH A FILE TO A MESSAGE

You can attach a file to a message you are sending. Attaching a file is useful when you want to include additional information with a message.

ATTACH A FILE TO A MESSAGE

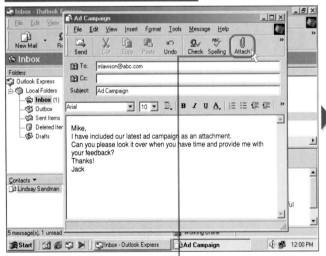

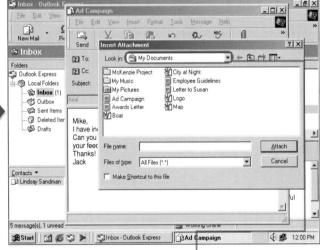

1 To create a message, perform steps 1 to 5 starting on page 274.

2 Click **Attach** to attach a file to the message.

Note: If the Attach button does not appear in the window, you need to enlarge the window to display the button. To resize a window, see page 17.

■ The Insert Attachment dialog box appears.

■ This area shows the location of the displayed files. You can click this area to change the location.

What types of files can I attach to a message?

You can attach files such as documents, images, programs, sounds and videos to a message. The computer receiving the message must have the necessary hardware and software to display or play the file.

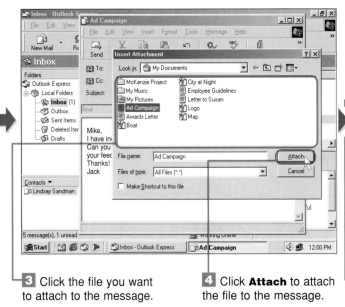

3 Click the file you want to attach to the message.

4 Click **Attach** to attach the file to the message.

■ This area displays the name and size of the file you selected.

■ To attach additional files, perform steps **2** to **4** for each file you want to attach to the message.

5 Click **Send** to send the message.

OPEN AN ATTACHED FILE

You can easily open a file attached to a message you receive.

Before opening an attached file, make sure the file is from a reliable source. Some files may contain viruses, which can damage the information on your computer.

OPEN AN ATTACHED FILE

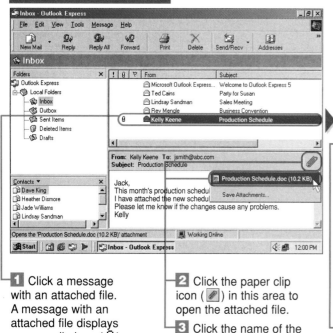

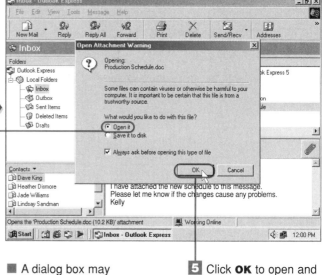

1 Click a message with an attached file. A message with an attached file displays a paper clip icon (📎).

2 Click the paper clip icon (📎) in this area to open the attached file.

3 Click the name of the file you want to open.

■ A dialog box may appear, asking if you want to open or save the file.

4 Click **Open it** to open the file (○ changes to ⊙).

5 Click **OK** to open and display the contents of the file on your screen.

284

DELETE A MESSAGE

You can delete a
message you no
longer need. Deleting
messages prevents
your folders from
becoming cluttered
with messages.

DELETE A MESSAGE

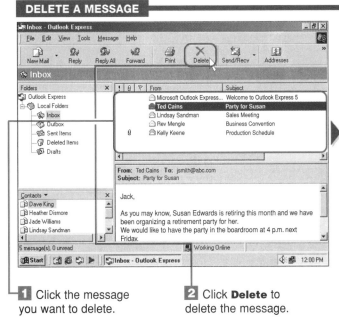

1 Click the message
you want to delete.

2 Click **Delete** to
delete the message.

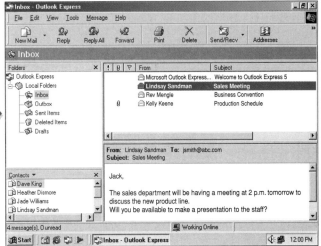

■ Outlook Express
removes the message
from the current folder
and places the message
in the Deleted Items
folder.

*Note: Deleting a message
from the Deleted Items folder
will permanently remove the
message from your computer.*

ADD A NAME TO THE ADDRESS BOOK

You can use the address book to store the e-mail addresses of people you frequently send messages to.

Selecting a name from the address book helps you avoid typing mistakes in an e-mail address, which can result in a message being delivered to the wrong person or being returned to you.

ADD A NAME TO THE ADDRESS BOOK

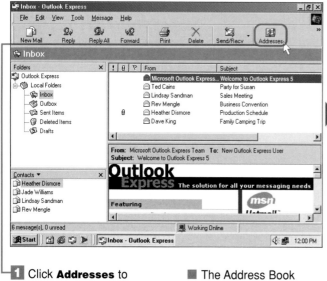

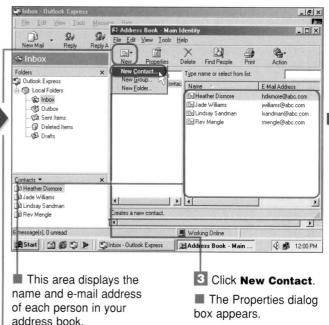

1 Click **Addresses** to display the address book.

■ The Address Book window appears.

■ This area displays the name and e-mail address of each person in your address book.

2 Click **New** to add a name to the address book.

3 Click **New Contact**.

■ The Properties dialog box appears.

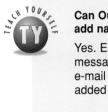

Can Outlook Express automatically add names to my address book?

Yes. Each time you reply to a message, the author's name and e-mail address are automatically added to your address book.

Do I have to open my address book to display the names in the address book?

In the Outlook Express window, the Contacts list displays the name of each person in your address book. You can quickly send a message to anyone in the Contacts list. To use the Contacts list to quickly send a message, see page 275.

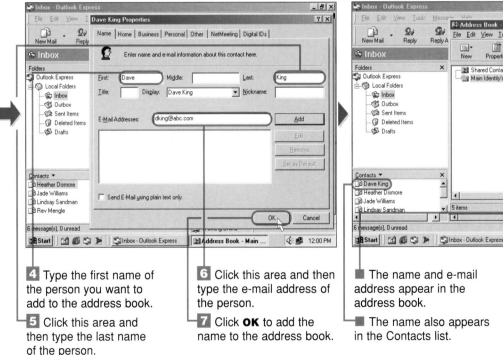

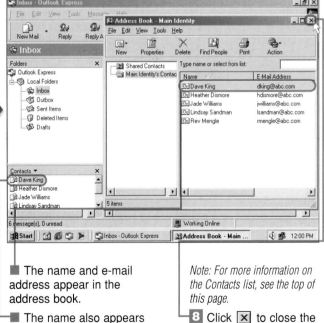

4 Type the first name of the person you want to add to the address book.

5 Click this area and then type the last name of the person.

6 Click this area and then type the e-mail address of the person.

7 Click **OK** to add the name to the address book.

■ The name and e-mail address appear in the address book.

■ The name also appears in the Contacts list.

Note: For more information on the Contacts list, see the top of this page.

8 Click ☒ to close the Address Book window.

ADD A GROUP TO THE ADDRESS BOOK

You can add a group to your address book so you can quickly send the same message to every person in the group.

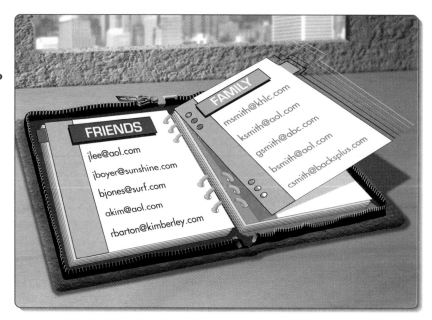

You can create groups for colleagues, friends and family members. When sending a message, you can select the group to send the message to every person in the group.

ADD A GROUP TO THE ADDRESS BOOK

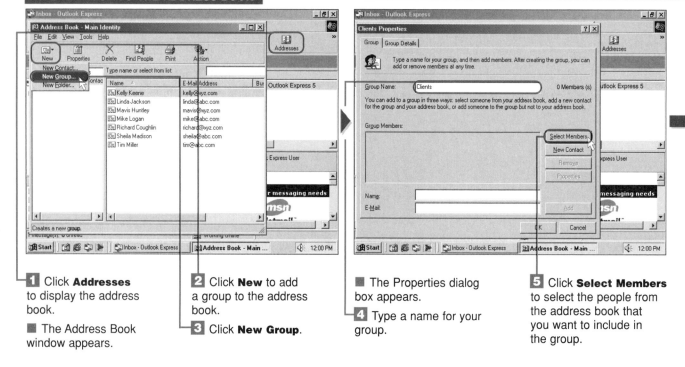

1 Click **Addresses** to display the address book.

■ The Address Book window appears.

2 Click **New** to add a group to the address book.

3 Click **New Group**.

■ The Properties dialog box appears.

4 Type a name for your group.

5 Click **Select Members** to select the people from the address book that you want to include in the group.

How can I send a message to a group?

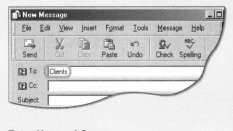

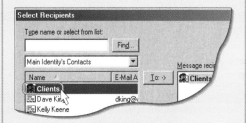

Enter Name of Group

When composing a message you want to send to a group, you can type the name of the group in the New Message window. To compose and send a message, see page 274.

Select Group from Address Book

If you cannot remember the name of the group you want to send a message to, you can select the group from your address book. To use the address book, see page 290.

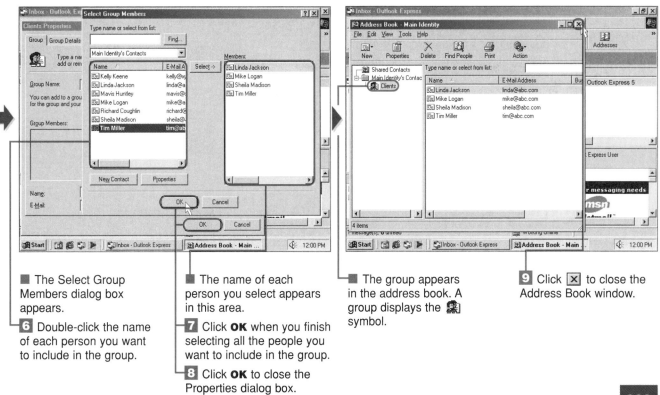

■ The Select Group Members dialog box appears.

6 Double-click the name of each person you want to include in the group.

■ The name of each person you select appears in this area.

7 Click **OK** when you finish selecting all the people you want to include in the group.

8 Click **OK** to close the Properties dialog box.

■ The group appears in the address book. A group displays the 🖼 symbol.

9 Click ☒ to close the Address Book window.

SELECT A NAME FROM THE ADDRESS BOOK

When sending a message, you can select the name of the person you want to receive the message from the address book.

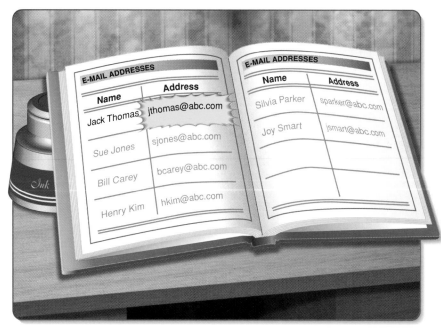

Selecting names from the address book saves you from having to remember e-mail addresses you often use.

SELECT A NAME FROM THE ADDRESS BOOK

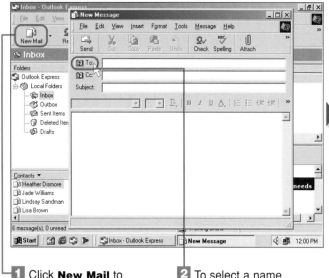

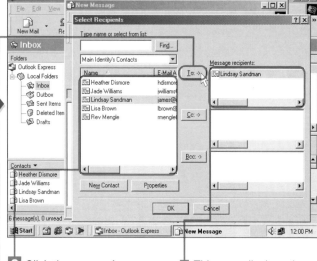

1 Click **New Mail** to create a new message.

■ The New Message window appears.

2 To select a name from the address book, click **To**.

■ The Select Recipients dialog box appears.

3 Click the name of the person you want to receive the message.

4 Click **To**.

■ This area displays the name of the person you selected.

■ You can repeat steps **3** and **4** for each person you want to receive the message.

How can I address a message I want to send?

To

Sends the message to the person you specify.

Carbon Copy (Cc)

Sends an exact copy of the message to a person who is not directly involved, but would be interested in the message.

Blind Carbon Copy (Bcc)

Sends an exact copy of the message to a person without anyone else knowing that the person received the message.

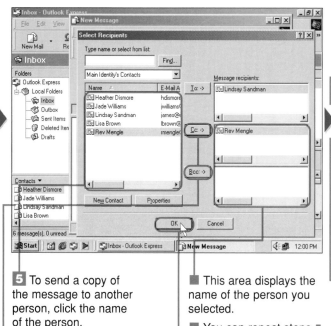

5 To send a copy of the message to another person, click the name of the person.

6 Click **Cc** or **Bcc**.

Note: For more information, see the top of this page.

■ This area displays the name of the person you selected.

■ You can repeat steps **5** and **6** for each person you want to receive a copy of the message.

7 Click **OK**.

■ This area displays the name of each person you selected from the address book.

■ You can now finish composing the message.

ADD A SIGNATURE TO MESSAGES

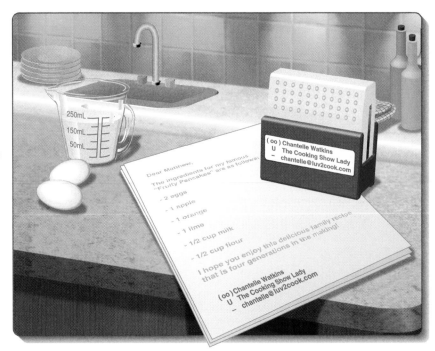

You can have Outlook Express add information about yourself to the end of every message you send. This information is called a signature.

A signature saves you from having to type the same information every time you send a message.

ADD A SIGNATURE TO MESSAGES

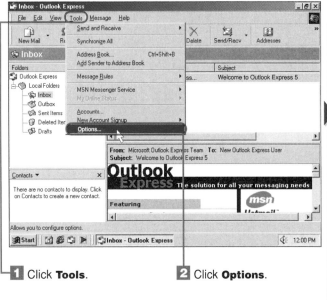

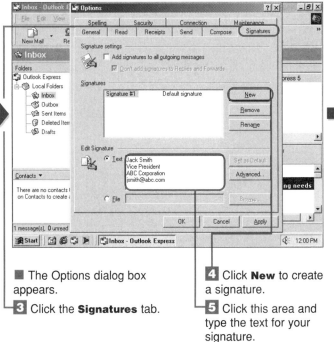

1 Click **Tools**.

2 Click **Options**.

■ The Options dialog box appears.

3 Click the **Signatures** tab.

4 Click **New** to create a signature.

5 Click this area and type the text for your signature.

What can I include in a signature?

A signature can include information such as your name, e-mail address, occupation, favorite quotation or Web page address. You can also use plain characters to display simple pictures in your signature. As a courtesy to people who will receive your messages, you should not create a signature that is more than four or five lines long.

Scott Kehoe
Sales Manager
ABC Corporation
skehoe@abc.com

(_@_)
M
_M_
⌐ ⌐ Jill Martin

Sarah Van Slyke
To be or not to be,
that is the question.

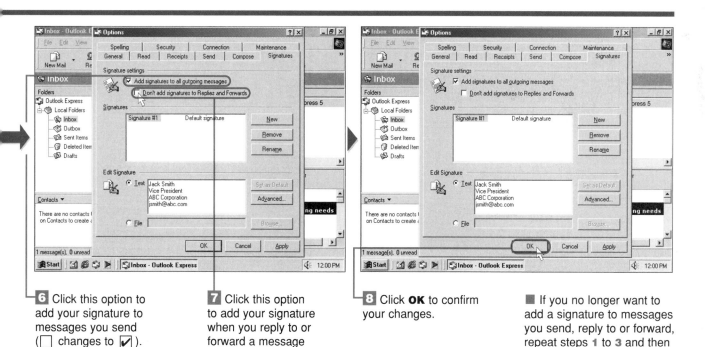

6 Click this option to add your signature to messages you send (☐ changes to ☑).

7 Click this option to add your signature when you reply to or forward a message (☑ changes to ☐).

8 Click **OK** to confirm your changes.

■ If you no longer want to add a signature to messages you send, reply to or forward, repeat steps **1** to **3** and then perform step **6** (☑ changes to ☐ in step **6**). Then press the Enter key.

INDEX

INDEX

INDEX

INDEX

INDEX